In Business Together

Negotiating the intimate relationship and the business partnership

- HANNAH COLLINS -

In Business Together:
Negotiating the intimate relationship and the business partnership

Copyright © Hannah Collins. First published 2020

Hannah Collins asserts the moral right to be identified as the author of In Business Together:
Negotiating the intimate relationship and the business partnership

Copyright © Witchwork Publishing
All rights reserved. No part of this publication may be reproduced, stored in a retrieval system or transmitted in any form or by any means, mechanical, electronic, photocopying, recording or otherwise, without the prior written permission of the author.

This book and any associated materials, suggestions and advice are intended to give general information only. The author expressly disclaims all liability to any person arising directly or indirectly from the use of, or for any errors or omissions in this book. The adoption and application of the information in this book is at the readers' discretion and is his or her sole responsibility.

In Business Together:
Negotiating the intimate relationship and the business partnership
Hannah Collins
ISBN: 978-0-646-81708-8
Edited by Karen Crombie at Exact Editing
Author photograph: Image Technique Photography: Philippe Flatt

This book is dedicated to Mary-Anne Muir,
Who has been with me since childhood.

Table of Contents

Chapter 1	Hannah and Heather	7
Chapter 2	We Meet Online	15
Chapter 3	We Buy A Business	27
Chapter 4	Catastrophe For Our New Business	39
Chapter 5	Our Commitment Ceremony	47
Chapter 6	Being a Dog Groomer	55
Chapter 7	We Make A Plan	67
Chapter 8	We Need Dog Walkers	83
Chapter 9	Caring For The Cat	99
Chapter 10	Our Glue	111
Chapter 11	We Sell Up	123
Afterword		133
Soul Scribbling		137
Author Q&A		139
Acknowledgements		145
Resources		147
About the Author		151
Connect with the Author		155

1

Hannah and Heather

"And how much is that going to cost?"

I don't stop typing. I don't look up. I can tell from the tone of Heather's voice she's already made up her mind. She doesn't like spending money on non-essentials and a counsellor definitely falls into that category.

It's me who wants to talk with someone, it's me who is ready to spend time and money, it's me who is frightened, not sleeping and when I do drift off, it's me having nightmares. I'm the one not sure of what we are planning to do. My real fear is that we have sacrificed our intimate relationship for a successful business.

"I think we need to talk to someone on the outside," I say slowly, as if this will win her over. "I want to talk to someone on the outside, someone impartial, who can help us sort through the issues of selling the business, selling the house, leaving Sydney and moving interstate." There. I've said it, stated out loud what has been buzzing around inside my head for weeks.

"I don't see the problem,' says Heather. "This is something we've wanted, talked about, planned for years. Why do you need to talk with someone now?"

I've stopped typing, my fingers tensed, frozen over the keyboard. "Because I'm not coping."

There's nothing I can say that's going to sound rational and credible. My head's full, trying to make order out of everything that needs to be done; packing, cleaning, organising a garage sale, signing up with a real estate agent, the open homes, trying to say goodbye to everyone. And then the long drive down to Victoria, with the cat and four Chihuahuas. It's like I'm coming down with the flu; I'm struggling with a blocked head, cold sweats, running a temperature, and the dream we have been holding onto is becoming a nightmare.

I toss and turn as night after night, featureless faces loom menacingly over me. I walk down dark, unknown streets where small, sinister houses crouch and wait. I need my phone. I need help. My heart begins to race, my breathing becomes quick and shallow. I toss the cushions off the couch, open and close cupboard doors, looking, looking. And then it's there in my hand, my phone, but what number do I call? I can't remember. I start the search again, looking for my address book, where can it be? My hand is growing hot, burning and as I stare down, my phone begins to melt, dripping through my spread fingers like melted butter.

"I'm not coping," I say again, remembering the dreams. "I need to talk with someone." I know I'm repeating myself and I can hear the desperation in my voice. It's not really about selling the business or selling the house or moving to another state. I'm worried about our relationship, how it will look, how it will feel - will we even have one when we've sold the business?

I don't know how to explain it, this sudden vague fear in the pit of my belly. It's as if I can't separate the relationship and the business. I can't see them clearly as two distinct shapes. They've morphed and become one, a mirror and its reflection, a figure and its shadow. They're bound so tightly I can't tell where the intimacy of our relationship ends, and the business partnership begins. It frightens me.

Our relationship, the way we are together, how we love and care for each other, has been defined and shaped by the ten years we have owned and run the business. A business that isn't a standard nine to five working week. We've been a business that offers our service seven days a week, 365 days a year. No weekends, no public holidays, no holidays of any kind, without working remotely on the laptop. Our relationship, our lives, have for a decade been determined by the business. And I'm beginning to think, what if, when we sell the business and extract ourselves from what has been normal all those years, we don't find our intimate relationship waiting for us?

"Who are we now?" I plough on, needing Heather to understand how I'm feeling. "We're not the same two women who met online and fell in love." Our desks are next to each other, against the short wall in the open plan kitchen/dining room/office. I swivel round in my office chair to face her. "We had a brief few weeks together when I moved in and then bought the business."

I see now how our first months when we'd been so happy to be together, so happy that finally everything had worked out alright after our disastrous beginning, had been crushed under the weight of our becoming new and inexperienced business owners. We had put aside all that romance, the dating, my sightseeing around Sydney, to work on our survival in the competitive world of home-based small business.

"We're the same people." Heather insists, leaning back in her own black swivel office chair. "We love each other, we're friends. If anything, we're better than when we met, stronger, we know each other, have learnt about ourselves and each other. What are you so worried about?"

"We made a promise to each other when we met," I say. "To have a different type of relationship. Do you remember?"

"You mean that book, about being independent and being equal. Of course I do. Well, we have, we are." Heather insists.

A friend had loaned me a book on intimate relationships and how to stop them from becoming enmeshed and strangling each other's personality, needs, dreams and creativity. The book had become a bible to me as I searched online for someone to talk to, someone to fall in love with, to have a functional, intimate, adult-to-adult relationship with. Although I was in my late fifties, I still hadn't had one of 'those' relationships. My relationships had always been co-dependent relationships, where I gave up my emotional needs to care for my partner's needs. It had been part of my addict personality and now, at twenty-odd years sober, I was keen to have a loving relationship where I didn't lose myself.

"What about when we sell up and move?" I keep pushing. Having started the conversation I'm loath to give it up. "What happens when we start our new life; is it going to be like these two desks, parallel lives, you outside in the garden shed, pottering around, planting fruit trees, growing carrots. Me in my writing room, study, office thing, catching glimpses of you through the window, waving, wishing we were sitting together inside, talking."

My big beef, wanting Heather to talk to me, wanting more than she can give. I want to talk more deeply than, "Hey, the carrots are doing well, the dogs love the extra backyard space, what a nice day." I want to know how she feels, what she is learning about herself as she plants cabbages and bakes bread. I want to hear about the creative process going on in her brain and what made her decide she wanted to grow carrots and cabbages and bake bread. I want to talk to her, to share my latest piece of writing, to know she's interested, to know I am heard and truly listened to. Isn't that what intimacy is also about? Not just the physical.

"You worry too much. I want the same things you want." Heather says, picking up her phone. "A bit of land for my garden and the animals to run around on. A room for your writing." She drifts off, her attention now on the small screen. I wait a moment and then turn back to the computer.

It's hard to keep her attention when we're talking about ideas, thoughts, feelings. Heather's a very practical woman; what she can see, touch, hold, carry - these things take her attention. She's what people used to refer to as a 'doing' person. Maybe it's her Virgo earthliness that makes her so different from the fire in my Leo natal chart.

I'm searching for a relationship counsellor online. I know what I want, I have a picture of her in my mind; a lesbian, local, with an up to date website, she writes about herself and her practice in good, clear writing, who posts regularly on her social media to a committed community. It's an instinct thing, I'll know intuitively when I've found the right one. Everything about her will match this idea I'm holding in my mind and that quiet, whispering voice will agree with me, or is the voice the one that will point me in the right direction? I've stopped trying to figure out 'the chicken or the egg' conundrum of that whispering voice.

I want Heather to come with me to talk to the counsellor. So often it is when I listen to Heather talk to other people that I truly learn what she is thinking and feeling. I tell her this, but she doesn't understand the issue. It's as if she feels safer talking to a stranger. It hurts. I don't want it to be that way when we sell up and move.

I listen to Heather telling clients that we want to move, sell the business, get out of the city. "We're not retiring," she explains. "Just starting the next phase of our life." She doesn't use the word retiring; that's for old people and Heather doesn't feel old. In fact, she's doing all she can to fend off old age, using a diet based on raw vegetables and a small amount of protein, plus regular exercise.

That's why moving is so important to her. She wants a large garden for vegetables, berry vines and fruit trees. Free-range chooks, maybe honeybees, possibly livestock, such as sheep and a pig. She wants to make her own sauerkraut, bake her own bread, bottle her own fruit and make jam. She wants to trade her extra veggies and bottled goods for other peoples' supplies and handcraft, be part of a community that fosters helping one another. She sees herself as being self-sufficient, off-grid, an eco-warrior.

I smile while she chats on about wind turbines, underground root cellars, solar panels, storage batteries and generators. I have my own dream; a studio, a study, my own space. There's a large wooden desk under a window with a view of the hills under a wide blue sky. There is a comfortable chair and a reading lamp. There's a stack of books on the coffee table at my elbow, with room for my favourite coffee mug. The far wall displays floor-to-ceiling books on wooden shelving. Attractive jars of coloured pens and pencils with accompanying colouring books are neatly arranged. Framed prints and photos are hung with precision around the room, bird nests, feathers, pretty stones, shells, beads, and mini-animal figurines are assembled on the window ledges. In this perfect setting, I will write ten books in ten years, filling the pages with my Wise Woman words.

2

We Meet Online

"Just talk to me."

She was so easy to talk to, this stranger in Sydney. Her bio had mentioned wanting someone other than her cat to share her bed and that had made me smile. So I had sent her a 'Smile'. A round, egg-yolk yellow, smiley face that you sent to someone you found interesting. It was the last sticker, on the last day of my subscription, the last time I would be on the site before I was done with online dating, and I sent a 'Smile' to Heather.

It was an odd experience reading a stranger's bio, looking at their photo, trying to see if there was something about them you connected with, and then the randomness of deciding whether or not to send them a 'Smiley Face Sticker'. Every day there were dozens of new bios, dozens of colour photos of women, standing square on or turned to the side, looking over their shoulder or through a mane of hair. They came in all shapes and sizes, all manner of dress and undress, smiling with confidence, staring back with eyes daring you to judge, criticise, find them unfriendly, unlovable.

There was something so sad, so needy about the daily pages of writing and photographs, I wanted to shower and change my clothes after half an hour. I felt like a voyeur going through someone's underwear drawer or dirty laundry basket. The endless scrolling past photo after photo seemed wrong, in a way that cruising a crowded bar had never seemed to me. It wasn't that it felt any less than a fresh 'meat market', but that the stories, the bitterness of broken hearts and dreams, starkly outlined on paper, seemed so much worse sitting in my bright sunny bedroom than chatting someone up in a dimly lit bar after two beers, long ago.

The next day, there it was - a big, round, egg-yolk yellow, smiley face from Heather. My last smiley face on the last day and I had one chance to send her my email address and see if she broke all the rules and emailed back.

"Just talk to me." She replied and so I did. Talking about being a house cleaner in Western Australian retirement villages. I wasn't too proud to clean old people's toilets, to vacuum through their two-bedroom apartments, wash their dishes, clean out their fridge and cupboards. I found it a pleasant way to spend my day, driving from gated community to gated community, chatting to returned servicemen and widows who were often housebound and as lonely as I was. It was my son who suggested I needed to get online.

Leaving New Zealand

I hadn't ever thought about leaving New Zealand and I wouldn't have when I did, if my youngest son hadn't married his partner and moved to Western

Australia. His invitation to join them came at a time when I wasn't happy. It wasn't anything in particular, but I felt like I was dissatisfied, merely hanging around waiting to die. I had a satisfying job managing a women's high fashion store with great staff and good remuneration. I had a rental close to the beach, a short drive to work and an hour commute into the city.

Australia was a culture shock. I'd grown up with the idea our two countries were similar, sisters joined through mutual language, the Queen, and shared history. I was familiar with Australia as seen on the television, the nightly news, or movies. I knew we were sporting rivals, had different accents, different money and were major tourists for each other's country.

As much as Australia was ostensibly the same, it was also different from New Zealand. The many variations were subtle, and difficult to put a finger on. I felt like a sailor coming back to a familiar shore, still with my sea legs; everything ever-so-slightly off-balance, the landscape undulating around me. The large country town seemed to be forever closing its doors and going home. Paying by cash, not card. Supermarkets operated between nine and five, there was very little choice for weekend brunch, no public transport and no Gay bars.

And that was my problem. With no official place to go, I was having trouble meeting lesbians and making friends. It wasn't that there were no gays; I saw them shopping in the supermarket, in the library with books under their arms, gathered in small groups drinking coffee, but I was new, not safe, and no one was willing to meet my eye.

I wasn't lonely, I wasn't homesick for New Zealand, yet I didn't want to be on my own. I wanted to be in a relationship. I wanted that mirrored reflection to see who I was. I didn't need someone to make me whole or complete me, but I wanted my opposite, someone social, someone who mixed freely and enjoyed being out and about as much as I enjoyed staying home. I believed I would grow best and finally learn about intimacy in a trusting and loving relationship. I was hoping I might find that in Australia.

While being a stranger was making it difficult to meet women and make friends, it was also fun to have a fresh start. I was free to be whoever I wanted, not that I didn't want to be myself. But any new friends would accept who I was, not judge me on my past, not make assumptions because they knew I had once been an alcoholic and drug addict, living in a van on the side of the street. To them I would have no past, I could be who I was from today. I had no intention of covering up my past; I believe we should talk to each other about the damage done to us. But I would be seen as a sober woman, not judged as a drunk. I would be employed as a trustworthy person, not pitied as a homeless, unemployable drug addict.

I'd been sober twenty-plus years, but I still hadn't had a functional, loving relationship with another adult. I hadn't had a relationship where I didn't put my life on hold and attend to the emotional and practical needs of my partner. I was quick to support and encourage their needs and goals, while abandoning my own. I seemed unable to maintain a clear, healthy boundary where they managed their needs and wants, and I saw to mine.

I felt I was running out of time, I was closer to sixty than fifty and I thought I might have waited too long, was too cynical, too old to change my habits. Yet I still wanted to experience intimacy without mistaking lust for love. I wanted to experience the security that would allow me to open fully to someone I trusted. I wanted to experience sexual pleasure without flashbacks, shame, and the trauma of my childhood sexual abuse shutting me down, making me dissociate or 'switch off'.

I wanted to reawaken that part of myself I'd pretended didn't exist, to break old patterns of behaviour and become brave enough to stay present, say what I wanted and take a risk. All my life I had settled for becoming what the other person wanted or needed. What made the other person feel comfortable. To make their life easier, I would hold my tongue, not speak out, not share my thoughts, my ideas, my opinions, my creativity, my skills, my experience and expertise. Always agreeing and saying yes, until the relationship was unhealthy and toxic.

I didn't have a picture in my mind of what this intimate relationship might look or feel like. I had a fuzzy idea from television and the movies, what I'd read or heard women talking about. As a child, I hadn't seen my parents being gentle and loving with each other. I was never told, "I love you," not by the adults who were supposed to protect me. I heard it from my grandfather.

Someone Beside The Cat To Share My Bed

It was fun talking to Heather. She told me about her redundancy and how she was going to go back to the buses, but at present she had a part-time driving job for Australia Post. She had a quaint Australian accent, a drawl when she pronounced her 'p's' and a way of ending her sentences at a higher pitch. I told her how that one line in her bio about having a cat on her bed had prompted me to send my last 'Smiley face' and that I had brought my cat, Cameo, with me when I moved to Australia.

What a difference it made, having a friend, someone to download with at the end of the day, someone to giggle with about the old ladies I met on the job. We swapped 'selfies' during the day, Heather driving around picking up mail from warehouses and offices, me cleaning bathrooms and hanging out washing.

Heather is looking over my shoulder reading as I type. "What are you writing about?" she says as she leans closer. "You've got a big smile on your face."

"I'm talking about how we met online and used to text each other and send selfie pictures when we were supposed to be working." I stop typing and lounge back in my chair. "I was remembering how much fun it was, how it brightened up my day, made everything seem easier and the day go quicker."

"Have you told that story about how you put your foot in the bucket of water when you were washing the floor at one of places in the retirement village, and because you were laughing so much, you tipped over the bucket and flooded the bathroom?"

"That was your fault, for sending that dirty text." I'd been so surprised by the sudden change from cheeky to sexual innuendo I'd stepped back without looking and put my foot in the bucket of hot soapy water. I nearly tripped over, I was laughing so hard, and only just managed to grab the hand basin to stop myself crashing to the floor.

"Then the old lady came in to find out what all the noise was about, and she wasn't happy about the mess or the noise. You know she complained to my boss." I shake my head, still smiling at the memory.

"Good times," smiles Heather, drifting back into the kitchen to make a cup of tea.

Indeed, they were good times and they had gone on for months and months. My routine was to get ready for work and then drive in from the coast where I was living and then, when I was within phone range, pull over and make my first call of the day. Heather, of course, had been up for hours because of the time difference. We'd chat and then we'd both go about our day. Each time either of us got a break we'd text. We'd have one last long talk in the evening.

We talked about everything, our family, our past lovers, the important relationships, the jobs we'd had. We shared our thoughts, our different political ideas, what we had in common and what we wanted in the future. We sent each other cards, flowers, jokes, funny pictures and the occasional sexy photo.

We never referred to what was happening between us as a romance, but it was. We didn't talk about our feelings as they related to each other, but we did share our views on the perfect relationship and how we'd both like to have one. It was like we were completely open and honest with each other while simultaneously ignoring the elephant in the room. We said things like, "I wish you were here," and "You're 3,934 kms away." We talked about the distance as a practical thing but not about whether we wanted to close the emotional distance.

Even in this funny, friendly, happy bubble, we had differences of opinion, we sometimes argued. I found Heather could be stubborn and judgemental, she had a temper, as did I. I remember having an argument over something while I was cleaning an old fellow's house. He was ex-army and sat next to the radio all day listening to the Greek news. I'd been so angry and upset at something Heather said that I told him I'd left some cleaning rags in the car and I was going to get them. I stormed out of the house, up the driveway and marched around and around the car, muttering about the bloody Sydney bitch.

While cleaning houses was paying the bills, it was also boring. Sure, knowing Heather and talking to her each day was entertaining but I needed something else to do. I started an online course to become a Life Coach. I enjoyed working with women one to one and while I didn't know anyone, I thought if I set up a small business maybe I could get involved in business networking or business organisations. It was a six-month course and so I got started.

With my plans to set myself up in business, I approached the bank for a business loan. I needed two thousand dollars to cover business cards, advertising, handout material and general start-up costs. The woman at the bank seemed very interested in my business idea even though she had no idea what a Life Coach was and why someone would want to talk to one. She smiled pleasantly while giving me a 'you're kidding' kind of look.

It seemed the bank would only lend me double what I needed and as she leaned across her desk in a secretive way, she said, "I'm sure you could find something to do with the rest of the money..."

"Yes, I'm going to buy a pair of green shoes I saw in the shoe shop window on my way here and then I'm going to book a return flight to Sydney. There's someone there I want to meet."

Flight Booked

You never saw two women more excited and so nervous, as Heather and I counted down the days, crossing off how many sleeps to go. Now the days dragged by, each day lasting a week. My son didn't want me to go to King's Cross; his mining mates had told him horror stories about the place. He wanted to know if I had enough money to stay in a hotel, just in case, and to make sure and call him if I needed to come home early. I think he had visions of his broken-hearted mother being mugged, or worse, in the underbelly of Australia's largest city.

"Heather?" I give her a call, as she's outside tending her pot plants. "What do you remember most about the day I flew into Sydney that first time to meet you?" I remember being frightened I wouldn't recognise her even though we'd been Skyping for months. I know I was nervous.

"I remember you were the last person off the plane and by then I was all sweaty and thinking you weren't even on the plane." She's standing in the doorway, holding a pair of secateurs.

"You were wearing that tiny flower-print shirt and jeans. Your face was flushed, and you looked scared." I start to laugh, "And you couldn't remember how to get out of the airport, and we seemed to wander round and round for ages, our arms around each other, just grateful that we were finally together."

"That's right, I was so uptight, and I didn't know what to expect and I'd been waiting in that lounge so long."

Heather leans against the glass sliding door staring at me but not really here.

I can tell by the glazed look on her face she's drifted off. "What else do you remember about our first meeting?"

"Well, I didn't have to see a counsellor as you did."

I'd missed that bit out in telling the story, but it's true, I did talk to a counsellor before I booked my flight to Sydney.

As I said, I'd drive each morning toward town until I got into mobile phone range, then I'd pull over and call Heather. One morning, an ordinary morning like all the other mornings over the months that I'd been doing this, I had a thought. I thought how I was feeling was falling in love. Crazy, not to be taken seriously, I scoffed and turned the key to start the car and get on with my day. But the thought and the feelings persisted, in fact, now I'd put a name to them they got stronger. It was a completely stupid idea, no one was going to fall in love with someone they had never met, it didn't happen, couldn't happen, so stop thinking about it.

I couldn't make sense of it, it wasn't rational, it wasn't logical, one didn't just fall in love with someone on the other side of a continent, especially if they had never laid eyes on them in the flesh. It couldn't be happening. I booked a session with a counsellor, knowing she would sort out what was happening, give me a reasoned and logical reason, tell me it was a romantic infatuation and it would eventually go away.

But that's not what she said. I described how I was feeling; warm and fuzzy, heart racing, a mixture of painful but also a bit high, excited with anticipation, tense and short-tempered while also feeling I could break all the rules and not care. A little out of control, actually. Well, sometimes a lot out of control.

I remember her laughing, it's stuck in my mind, her face humorously screwed up, and holding her hand over her mouth. I remember feeling offended and pissed off that she was making fun of me while I was being deadly serious.

"It's love, Hannah," she said, when she finally got her laughter under control. "It's how people feel, it's how I felt when I met my husband, it's normal, common even. You're feeling something perfectly normal. Congratulations, I hope you will be very happy."

I argued, I listed all the reasons why it couldn't be love. Firstly, I hadn't met this person in the flesh. Heather had stopped being Heather and become this third-person stranger who was causing me to be ridiculed by this professional for whom I was rapidly losing respect. I wasn't convinced but I did have more information about how people fall in love and how that might feel.

Rainbow City

Sydney was beautiful, with the harbour, the Opera House, the famous bridge, the ferries, the shops, the cafes and fine dining. I was the tourist and Heather my guide. She loved showing me around, she was in love with her city, I just wasn't sure she was in love with me. Sure, we were having fun, staying in bed late, walking around the tourist sights hand in hand, sneaking kisses and grinning like fifteen-year-olds.

But there was something off and it's hard to explain. I was with the woman I had spent months and months talking with on the phone, I knew her voice, the accent, laugh, and her temper but at the same time, the woman I was lying next to in bed wasn't her. There was Heather, the voice on the phone that I pictured in my mind, the woman I was pretty sure I was in love with. And there was this other woman with her physical body, her facial expressions, her mannerisms, body language, style of dress, way of eating, how she held her knife and fork. This second woman I didn't know, she was oddly unfamiliar, and it unsettled me, so from time to time I'd go down to the bedroom and call Heather on the phone so I could talk with my friend.

While I'd been pretty sure of how my telephone friend Heather felt, I wasn't so sure about this Heather, the one I was visiting for ten days in Sydney. The Sydney Heather was different. My discomfort about my feelings, being disconcerted about the two Heathers, my fear of being hurt or making a fool of myself gradually shut me down over the course of my time in Sydney. Having arrived excited and open-hearted, ready to throw myself into Heather's arms, wanting to be romantically swept off my feet, to be told I had her undying love, I was now feeling a little underwhelmed and a little let down. All my high hopes and 'in-love' dreams were crashing into reality. Heather wasn't acting as if she felt the same way I did, and my reaction was to run away, as far and fast as possible. So that's what I did.

At the end of ten days, having had a wonderful time, having enjoyed Sydney and the time I spent with Heather, I asked her to delete my number from her phone and to respect my need for no contact. I didn't want to be 'just a friend', to know she was seeing other women, to hear about her dating life. I wanted it to be cut and dried: our romance was at an end, it hadn't worked out, no hard feelings, goodbye.

3

We Buy A Business

"By the way, I'm selling my business."

It's a throwaway line, an afterthought, and at first, I wasn't sure I'd heard him correctly. I check back over my shoulder and catch his eye. He's grinning, body turned towards us, resting on one arm, and waving goodbye with the other. We'd been sitting in the shade under the trees, drinking coffee while he and Heather had a catch-up, but he hadn't mentioned the sale of his business once. So why now?

But before I have time to give it any more thought, there's that quiet, familiar little voice whispering in the back of my mind. *"You will buy the business."*

On one level I'm not shocked at all. I've lived with that quiet whisper all my life. It's the voice of my Inner World, my Inner Self, my intuition. It's a voice I recognise and pay attention to. It's like my internal guidance system. It's a combination of a voice in my mind and a feeling in the pit of my stomach. It's an alert, *this is important*, this is what is about to happen, so take notice. I've been aware of the voice since I was a child.

I don't talk about it much, I don't often tell people, they sometimes give me a weird look and I feel uncomfortable. Some people, especially women, understand and some even admit to having their own Inner Voice. I find that reassuring. It means I'm not alone. But when I do feel alone is when I'm trying to find other women who live from the Inside out. My Inner World is more important than my Outer World.

I know it can be difficult to understand. Imagine my surprise when I found out most people live from their Outer World and some don't even know they have an Inner World, an Inner Self. Heather was one of those people, with no idea what I was talking about when I told her my Inner Life was the way I lived. She didn't speak for a moment and I could visualise the wheels in her head whirling around - we were on the phone so I couldn't see her facial reaction. It was during the time we were chatting every day after meeting online.

Heather lives in the Outer World; she takes action and makes decisions when confronted by outside events. She likes the world she has built around her, her home, her car, her friends, her family, the things she owns and has placed around herself. This represents her security, these things.

I'm secure in my Inner World, I feel safe listening to my Inner Voice, my Inner Self. So when I hear that quiet whispering voice say; *"You will buy the business,"* my mind goes into overdrive. It's not easy to describe, there are pictures like having a dozen tabs open on your computer, there are the past experiences that relate to the pictures, memories, ideas, creative visions, experiences. There are a hundred opportunities buzzing around, as if someone spilled all the colours and shapes from a kaleidoscope. At the same time, all of this is beginning to form a pattern that resonates with my personality traits of organisation, planning, bringing control to the chaos and making To-Do lists.

I poke Heather in the ribs.

"How much do you think he wants?" She stares at me blankly. "The business," I say. "How much do you think he wants for his business?"

She hasn't heard him. She stops and turns back toward the trees where we had been sitting. He's still there, his partner beside him.

"You mean the dog grooming van?"

"Yes, the grooming van, it's up for sale."

"Well, we don't want it, not a dog grooming van."

I realise it's not going to be easy because neither Heather nor I can groom dogs, but it ticks all the boxes and while I don't continue the conversation, but fall in step as we walk back to the car, my mind is busy thinking and thinking.

A Life-Changing Accident

After I had visited Heather in Sydney, staying ten days in her home, I ended the budding romance. It was during this time, after I'd stopped all contact, that Heather had a terrible accident and blinded herself in her right eye.

It was just a bit of silly rivalry between dog-owning friends. They were a friendly bunch that met after work for a chat while their dogs ran around the park, sniffing and pissing. They'd been meeting for years and this time had a lively discussion about home-brewed ginger beer. Heather, not being a woman to back down from a challenge, especially when her skill is being questioned, accepted and went home to put down a batch of ginger beer.

I was told later she had been woken in the early hours of the morning by a popping noise. She said she knew immediately it was the ginger beer, and without stopping to dress or put on her glasses, she hurried down to the kitchen to save the exploding bottles. As she opened the cupboard door, a piece of flying glass penetrated her right eyeball. The operating surgeon told Heather later, she was lucky they hadn't just scraped the deflated eyeball out and thrown it in the bin, such was the damage.

Over the months we were estranged, Heather was either in hospital having another eye operation or in a waiting room so her eye could be checked and rebandaged. Everyone held out hope for a while but eventually, the damage proved to be too much, and Heather is now sadly blind in that eye.

The accident was to change Heather's life, not just because she was now blind in one eye and couldn't resume her career of nearly thirty years, but also because it brought us back together again. Heather had worked for State Transit on the buses for most of her working life. She had started at the bottom as a Clippy, then a driver and eventually as a depot supervisor. She'd worked all around Sydney at the small and the new depots until she was offered redundancy. She had no problem accepting the payout, as under State Transit rules she could reapply for her position in six months. She paid the money off her mortgage and settled into a part-time driving job until the compulsory twenty-four weeks were up.

Accepting she was blind in one eye was devastating news for Heather. To work for State Transit you need a heavy driver's licence, even if you no longer drove buses, and to gain the licence you needed full sight. Between opening that kitchen cupboard door and the flying piece of glass entering Heather's eye, all her future plans vanished, along with her income.

The positive side of this terrible accident unfolded when a friend helped Heather sign up on Facebook and my photo popped up, asking "Is this someone you know?"

Heather Needs A Job

"We could buy his business." It seems simple and straightforward to me. Maybe it was all my years in retail, but I didn't see it so much as buying a business as buying a brand. Under our brand name, we could sell pet products, dog shampoo and conditioner, flea treatment, problem skin solutions, brushes and combs, fancy neckties, collars and leads, rain jackets, printed tee-shirts and toys. Pet owners were always buying stuff for their pets. I could see the potential.

"Buying this business will tick all the boxes, give you everything you wrote on your list." It became obvious to me we were never going to find Heather a job if we went about it her way. She was trying to find something to match her skills and certificates, and she was a Certified Trainer. She looked at other government jobs, the prison service, and being a trainer in the corporate world. But nothing was working. I suggested writing a list of how she'd love to spend her day at her ideal job; where would she be, what would she be doing? The results were amazing.

She didn't want to go back into an office, in middle management, answering to a boss, following department rules and regulations. She liked the idea of being her own boss, having flexibility, maybe working outdoors, gardening, or with animals. She didn't particularly like working alone; she enjoyed having company and someone to talk to.

"You know all the doggy people in the park and they're always saying how well-behaved Alex is. You're good with animals." Heather and her brown staffy Alex were well known in the dog park. "I bet they'd support you if you bought the grooming business; they'd be only too happy to have you handling their dogs."

I have a total blank about the next few weeks when it comes to remembering any discussions we had about buying the business. I'm sure we must have talked more and probably frequently, I'm a bit of a nagger. But I can't recall anything specific. I had learnt by then that Heather needed time to make a decision; after all, it took her six months to recognise she was in love with me.

I make up my mind quickly, in a restaurant it's a quick look through the menu and - boom - decision made. Heather needs to read the menu from cover to cover several times, to make up and change her mind a few times, and then at the last minute change it again before she orders. I've stopped letting waiters hover at the table, notebook and pencil in hand. I tell them

I'll wave when we're ready. Maybe it was like that when it came to buying the business. Maybe it was spending that much money.

"Heather..?" Maybe she remembers. "I can't remember what you were thinking about when it came to deciding whether to buy the business. I want to write it in the book. Was it spending that much money?"

"No, it was losing the house. If it all went wrong I was frightened I'd lose the house." She's in her yellow apron, arms full of vegetables for tonight's salad. "I was scared we wouldn't be able to do it, manage it, and I'd be forced to sell the house to pay off the debt."

That's right, it all comes back to me, the constant fear of losing the house. It was like the 'For Sale' sign was already up blinking on and off like a hotel sign; one minute we were safe, the next we were losing the house. It went on for months, maybe years. Heather lying awake in the middle of the night worrying, me snoring quietly beside her. I didn't have any of her concerns, I was supremely confident it would all work out. Maybe that's a little bit of my Leo arrogance and a big bit of my strong belief in my intuition.

"And you kept saying, we wouldn't lose the house because we were both hard workers, born with the fifties work ethic." She's resting against the stainless steel sink. "That the business had been successful for over six years and he'd done all the hard work, established the clients and worked out all the problems."

"Well, you did need a job." I point out. "And I thought if you had to retrain at something, why not as a dog groomer? I knew we'd both had experience in management and dealing with staff. I'd had those ten years handling horses and dogs aren't much different; at least they're lighter on your toes if they stand on your foot."

I gaze at Heather. She's ordinary in every way, a redhead with fair skin and freckles, short in the body, long in the leg. Dressed in jeans and a tee-shirt. Red framed glasses.

"Maybe I just let you talk me into it," she says, grinning. "You know your tendency to nag. But you were right. What else was I going to do? Even though I was scared, it was a mutual decision and it was something we could do together." She turns back to chopping vegetables for dinner. "As you always say, it wasn't a random meeting in the park that day. It was fate and meant to be."

The Handover

The week before Christmas is the busiest in the dog grooming calendar, with every dog owner wanting their pup looking its best for the holidays. Heather spent the first week standing at the back of the van trying to take in the overload of information and getting her first taste of what dog grooming was all about. There was instruction on how to use the washtub, how to hold them to lift the dogs on and off the grooming table, her first try of the electric clippers and learning every blade size for each coat type. She spent the evenings poring over the ring binder of breed clips.

On Christmas Eve, after the last dog was given a doggy treat and had a Christmas bandana tied around its neck, Heather was handed the van keys, given a peck on the cheek and congratulated as the new owner. On the passenger's seat of the van was a battered box of client information sheets with house keys attached to the corners. We were about to spend our first Christmas driving around the empty suburbs caring for our clients' pets.

"Do you think we had any idea what we were in for, that first Christmas?" I ask Heather. She's sitting at her desk now, watching a video on how to bake bread.

"NO!" She's been trying to bake the perfect loaf of sourdough. 'We had no idea what we were doing. All I remember is walking in and out of homes, feeding cats, trying not to lose the owners' keys, and being so tired I think we went to bed before nine every night."

"I spent every day doing three-point turns in the narrowest streets. Trying to follow GPS instructions, always turning left when I should have been turning right." Part of my dyslexia is to mix up left and right. When I'm driving, Heather taps my left arm for the left turn.

"Well, you'd only been in Sydney, what, two or three months? No wonder you didn't know your way around. But you soon learnt, didn't you?" She takes a moment to look away from her bread-baking video to give me a cheeky grin. "Remember that time when you called me, lost, but you said there was a dead-looking tree covered in real gold? I still can't work out how you managed to get yourself into the middle of the city."

The elation we felt as new business owners, of having the big, white grooming van with its colourful logo splashed all over its sides, was quickly subdued by the anxiety of finding the right address in the maze of apartment blocks. I'd never experienced anything like it. I'd open the entrance gate and spread out before me was a small city of looming towers, with a hundred windows and dozens of balconies.

I hardly think about putting a key in a lock, opening the door and walking into a client's house now, but back then I found the towering blocks very intimidating and being lost became the new norm. I met a lot of new people whilst wandering around with a client's details in my hand, a work bag over my shoulder containing a roll of black poo bags, cleaning cloths, a mini plastic brush and pan, and a Christmas business card. All vital things I found I needed on the job.

The actual job of caring for the client's cat wasn't difficult, I'd done that all my life. What was exhausting that first Christmas was getting used to walking through an empty home with all the evidence of a family celebration; a Christmas tree with flashing lights, piles of wrapped presents, strung-up decorations, Christmas cards on the mantelpiece, the desk, the window ledges, the benches, and occasionally *everything* Christmassy on display, right down to the themed cat's bowls.

I was never completely sure there wouldn't be anyone home, so I'd sing out 'hello' several times, and I still do. Both myself and a client have been surprised by each other. And then there are those awkward times when a client has been in the shower, hears a noise and comes out to investigate. It's no laughing matter; I've seen too many naked people in my ten years as a pet sitter.

It's unnerving at times to be searching through a stranger's home for the cat food and litter trays. To need cleaning equipment to sweep or mop up after a cat is sick. Everyone keeps cat food, spoons, and cleaning cloths in different places. I love it best when the client takes the time to give us full instructions, from 'the key sticks and you need to put your whole body weight against the door to get it to open', to where and how the cat is fed. I've kept the best-decorated, most meticulous instruction sheets, hoping to publish them when I write about my ten years in the pet industry, feeding and caring for other people's pets.

The worst aspect of that first Christmas was coming to terms with the people who either didn't have the time or didn't care about the state they left their house in. Unwashed dishes in the sink, the remains of their last meal on plates left on the kitchen bench. I've never become used to the stench of litter trays that hadn't been emptied for a week or more, or bags of rubbish left indoors, even when the client planned to be away for the weekend or longer. The state of uncleanliness of the house, especially the kitchen and bathroom. It's an aspect of our business that I've never gotten used to or understood.

At one end of the spectrum, the grand apartments with fine-china pet bowls and colour coordinated pouches of cat food in coloured trays marked 'breakfast' and 'dinner'. Some cats ate the finest cuts of beef, while others had the cheapest on-sale product from the local supermarket. There were apartments and houses that looked like a special edition from 'Home and Garden' and others that looked and smelled like a student flat where it was always someone else's turn to do the housework.

New Year

We double our prices on public holidays. We don't charge any extra for our weekend work. The ten to fourteen days over the Christmas New Year festive period is to cover the drop in work from mid-January through February and the start of the school year. Our business can be a bit famine or feast and it's important to understand the flow of work over the full year, where the public and school holidays fall and to plan for them accordingly.

We weren't thinking like that at the end of that first holiday season. We were just thankful for a breather after working fifteen days in a row. I'd learnt a lot about the suburban street layout but was still dependent on the GPS to get around. Heather taught me how to drive the van, as I was to take over when she left for her four weeks down south and her grooming course. It seemed we no sooner took a breath and caught up on our sleep, than things changed again.

Dog grooming had been cancelled until Heather came back from her grooming course. I was to manage dog washing and driving the big van, plus take the three dog walks each week and the pet sitting. Our booking system was an appointment book and pencil, invoices were basic, and we banked all the cash once a week. I was on my own. I had the house to myself plus Alex the dog, Heather's cat Henry and my cat Cameo. Heather and I were back to phone calls and text.

4
Catastrophe For Our New Business

"HELP, call an ambulance!"

My first thought was; this doesn't look right. My left foot is pointing in the wrong direction. I try to take stock of my situation, I'm sitting on the bottom step of the stairs from the upstairs bedroom to the hall, headed for the front door. I have a suitcase still clenched in each hand, my glasses have been knocked to the floor, but I can't see them.

I close my eyes. It all happened so fast, I remember slipping, being aware of the pain in my foot, but don't remember landing hard on my bottom. The pain is blinding.

Heather says I screamed and screamed. "You did; you think you screamed once but you didn't stop screaming, it just went on and on. I had time to run out from the kitchen, see you sitting on the bottom step, the sickening sight of your foot at right angles to your leg, run back to the kitchen to get the phone, ring triple zero, talk to the operator to send an ambulance and then kneel down and start talking to you. You were still screaming."

"Well, it hurt!"

The weekend had been my idea. Heather was down south at the dog grooming course and over the four weeks, she had been travelling back home on the weekends. On her last weekend away I thought it would be nice if I drove down to her. It would give me a chance to meet the other new groomers in Heather's class, plus be introduced to the amazing world-class professional groomer and dog show judge who was running the course. The owners of the B&B where Heather was staying were friends from the dog park, who had taken a 'tree-change', and we were all looking forward to a good catch up.

Saturday was fun, the small town was a tourist mecca and I'd bought earrings, Heather had found a gardening centre and I was to transport her new plants home with me the next day. Dinner was wonderful, as one of our hosts was an amazing cook, they'd invited the tutor, too, and as we all had dogs, the conversation had been lively with lots of funny doggy stories.

Sunday afternoon I was packing to drive back to Sydney. Heather was in the kitchen preparing her new plants for the journey and we were both relieved that in one week, the course would be over, and we'd be back home together.

It must have been a slow day in the little tourist town because over the next thirty minutes not one, but four ambulances arrived, one after another, plus a lone 'ambo' in an SUV, filling the driveway and parking on the front lawn. It was all pretty standard, routine, so one woman attended to me and the rest stood around talking. I was given 'the green whistle' to suck on for pain relief and placed on a stretcher. At the hospital, I was seen by a doctor, had an x-ray, my ankle was bandaged, and I was taken up to a ward to await surgery the following day. The surgeon wasn't available on Sunday for non-urgent cases and my broken tibia and fibula could wait, apparently. The following day the ankle was set with plates and screws and I was told I'd be off my feet for three months.

This was a disaster for our new business. Heather had one more week on her dog grooming course, I was supposed to be holding down the fort, washing and walking dogs, managing the office and the pet sitting. The accident came at the worst possible time - how on earth were we going to manage for three months? It seemed before we had even begun we had failed. It would take several months before we realised that this unfortunate event would, in fact, give me time to build the foundation for our business that would support us for the next ten years.

Heartbreak

But before I tell you how my broken ankle saved us from losing the business, I need to tell you how Heather and I eventually got back together again.

I had spent ten days with Heather in Sydney and then went back home. It was a terrible time; it felt like we'd had months and months of sun and warmth and fun and then everything was hidden behind a big, black, cold cloud. Work wasn't fun. I missed the texts, the jokes, the chatting and fooling around. Life seemed sterile and boring, a drab painting in monochrome after a festival of colour. I dragged myself from house to house, trying to find some pleasure in cleaning microwaves and windows. I'd ploughed ahead with my Life Coaching business idea and had a couple of women from work as guinea pigs; one was trying to quit smoking and the other wanted help dealing with the fall out with her sister.

I did have two special friends, a New Zealander and her Aussie husband. They propped me up as I mourned for my broken heart. They allowed me to wallow in what might have been my anger at Heather for not meeting my expectations, my self-indulgent misery, and my self-deprecating humour at my stupidity. It was the place I ran to when I was sick of myself, when I felt like the comfort of a home-cooked meal, or when I simply needed a shoulder to cry on. They were my lifeline.

I changed jobs, went back into retail management, started my little coaching business, moved into a larger flat, made friends with the neighbours, had a favourite cafe, pâtisserie, health food store and video shop. I was starting to find my feet, get comfortable, and had finally made contact with a small local group of lesbians who meet weekly for a friendly pot-luck. And then out of the blue, came a message from Heather.

It had been over six months and while it might have been the most wildly romantic thing in those first few weeks, it now came as a complete shock. For a moment I thought I might have a heart attack, I couldn't breathe, and then in typical blunt Hannah fashion, I responded by saying. "If you just want to know what the weather is like in WA, f*#@k off!"

I know, I know, after all that time of bleeding with the pain of being in love and not having it reciprocated, here I was driving her away before she had a chance to speak. I rang my trusty New Zealand friend and breathlessly told her Heather had sent a message.

She counselled caution and reminded me of how much pain I had been in over the last half a year, how many tears I'd shed, how unhappy and upset I had been. And then she laughed. "Too late - I can hear it in your voice, all has been forgiven, so, how soon are you moving to Sydney?"

She was right. I took a deep breath and told Heather my feelings hadn't changed and if hers had, she'd better get herself over here within the next forty-eight hours or it was all off again. She arrived the next day.

It was a wonderful reunion and the more so because we had both declared our feelings and I felt on firm ground. I felt giddy and light-headed and joyous and relieved. We walked along the beach making plans, making promises, talking about a future together, trying to work out how that would look. I had a new job, new twin granddaughters, a two-year lease, a new fridge and washing machine. Heather had hospital appointments for her damaged eye, an elderly parent, family and work. We were at an impasse; neither of us wanted to move.

At the end of ten days, we had decided to try a long-distance arrangement, each of us taking turns on the long-distance flight. It seemed workable and all either of us were prepared to do at that moment. I made a joke about tattooing 'She's Mine' on Heather's forehead and learnt how much she disliked 'inking'. I did a quick mental count of my tatts - oh well, nobody's perfect.

I was expecting phone calls on Mother's Day, after all, I have two sons. It was the third call that threw me; I was not required at work that morning. It was a shock until Heather told me to sell the car, put the furniture in storage, find someone to take over the lease and she'd meet me off the plane. The decision was made.

Working On The Business

I'm fully dressed, propped up with pillows on the bed, plastered leg resting on two cushions. I have the laptop open on my knees and I'm reading the client details and personal information from the handwritten pages I've taken out of the battered box we'd received at the handover.

Heather has now taken on all the physical work, dog grooming, dog walking and pet sitting. I'm going to be off my feet for at least three months, but I have to do something. I decide the client records seem the most logical place to start. It had occurred to me that some of these clients may not be using our services now or maybe the details weren't current. We don't know how many clients we have, and we don't know which of our services they use.

I've never used a computer for anything more than the basics and this is going to be a 'learn as you go' exercise. I need somewhere to put all our client details so we can move from this outdated paper system to a computerised system. I choose an email database and an accounting system. It's labour-intensive because I don't know how to use the computer properly and I don't know any short cuts. To begin, I call the clients to find out if they are still using our service, to explain we have bought the business, and to update their personal and pet information. At the end of the week, I've shredded more pages than I've added to our new databases.

When I do find an active client, I divide them into which service they use, dog grooming, dog walking, pet sitting. I'm beginning to create order out of chaos, I'm starting to feel comfortable using the laptop and I've discovered the wonder that is the World Wide Web. I'm side-tracked by the ability to find and read all kinds of information about small business, how to get started, what you need and how you can pay a subscription and join all types of groups. I feel as if I've walked into a secret world, one that has all the questions and the answers about running a home-based pet services business. I'm elated. Every day I leave my housebound body behind and dive into the magic land of the internet, jumping from website, to blog, to page, to newsletter, eagerly soaking up information as if I've never learnt anything in my life. Happy, I'm so happy. My mind is on fire, I'm alert and fully in my power in a way my dyslexia has never allowed me to be.

I start a list of things to do and then start another list and then another. There's so much to do. I need a newsletter. I need social media. I need to sign up for Facebook and Pinterest and Instagram. I need to update the business website. It's old fashioned and the cartoon animals make it look like Disneyland, when I think we should have a more professional profile. I study more websites and make another list.

My fingers couldn't keep up with my thoughts. I envisioned how the business would be with a database, a marketing program, a rewards program, an updated scheduling system with a calendar. We needed a budget, a marketing plan, and to find other businesses like ours, not just in the pet industry, but with women who also ran home-based businesses.

I'm energised and enthusiastic. I love learning, exploring, discovering and making things happen. I feel a sense of freedom, of having no limits, no boundaries as to what I can do. It's the opposite of how I felt growing up, how I felt at school. I am dyslexic and back then it was not known or understood. I was called dumb, stupid, lazy, slow and unwilling to apply myself. I often received physical punishment in front of the class and at home for not trying harder, for being insolent. But now I found I wanted to learn, I wanted the business to succeed. I hadn't been able to help financially to buy the business, but maybe this was my way, my contribution. If I could learn to run the business professionally, I wouldn't feel so guilty, I wouldn't feel I had pushed Heather into something that put her home in jeopardy.

I was so busy being happy and enjoying my newfound knowledge, I didn't notice that Heather wasn't happy. It didn't occur to me that my enthusiasm mightn't be shared. I was so busy, bursting with all I wanted to tell her and show her, to impress her, that I didn't stop to think or find out what was happening for her. All I knew was she came home tired each night and left again in the morning. I was so caught up in my joyful bubble I wasn't aware of everything about her situation, her feelings, and how she was coping.

This lack of awareness, of knowledge and understanding, would have terrible consequences for our intimate relationship and our business partnership. But I wouldn't learn that for many years.

5

Our Commitment Ceremony

"I don't want to wait ten or twenty years."

Our first anniversary was just around the corner. A year, twelve months, 365 days. And in that time so much had happened, the death of Heather's mother, buying the business, going back to Western Australia and selling up all the furniture I'd put in storage. Now here we were, sitting together in bed reminiscing, my ankle still in plaster, the grooming van parked outside, Heather's dog Alex and my cat Cameo curled up beside their respective owners.

"I don't see the point of proving we can make a go of our relationship and then making some type of social commitment to the fact. We didn't say, look we'll pay for the business in five years when we know it worked. We bought the business and then got working. Well, I feel the same way about our relationship. We make a commitment to make it work, not make a commitment when we know it works."

In Business Together

Heather is not saying anything. She's patting Alex on the head and one thing I've learnt in the nearly twelve months of living with her, is that I have to be patient. She takes a while to think things through, to process. I have no idea what she's thinking or how she processes her decisions. That's still a complete mystery to me. I know what I'm asking is coming from my insecurity. It's about trust. It's about stating I feel different. I feel different about this woman, about this relationship; it's special and I want everyone to know, understand and support this difference.

It's about being a lesbian and not having a formal way of making public how we feel about each other. It's about being seen as *less than* a heterosexual couple. That as a same-sex couple we have no right to expect society to uphold our love for each other, to support and respect our relationship. I've been called promiscuous because I have been in several relationships. It's commonly thought all gays are unable to have a lasting relationship, that we're fickle, and our relationships are about sex, not love. That we are somehow less than heterosexuals, immoral and undeserving of human rights. Of being married.

It's not that I believe in the institution of marriage, I think politically and historically it's been a bad deal for women, but what other way do we have to show friends and family that with this relationship, we have found what everyone wants; love and a desire to make a commitment to be a solid, foundational part of society, with all the rights, privileges and respect that is due.

I've attended my sons' weddings, I would like them to attend mine.

"Yes."

Our Commitment Ceremony

"Yes?"

"Yes. I was a bridesmaid for my sister, and I've been invited and gone to family weddings. I once flew to America to be at my nephew's wedding and that was his second marriage. Yes, let's have a wedding."

I'm too excited to correct her, to point out we can't have a wedding, but as we throw ourselves together in a big hug and Alex starts barking and the cat leaps off the bed. I throw caution to the wind about my broken leg, I'm too happy to do anything else but enjoy the moment.

Creating The Invitations

We are wandering around the speciality stationery store and while Heather remains on track I've been taken over by my fascination and addiction to all things paper, notebook and pen. I'm in my element, I rub my fingers over the notebook covers, I sniff the pages, I touch the journals and diaries and finger the cards and the paper and the pencils and pens. I'm mesmerised by the flower and glitter and gold leaf of the pencil cases, the little cardboard box pen holders, the endless array of colour card and . . .

"What about this?" Heather is holding up several different coloured cards and I'm brought back to the present. Later a friend will say, "I bet you made the invitations, they were so lovely, simple but elegant." But no, Heather threw herself into making the invitations, writing the words, deciding who should be present outside of the immediate family.

We shopped for rings, for wedding outfits and shoes. We made decisions about the time, the marriage celebrant, the photographer, filling out the documentation for the City of Sydney registry, the music, the menu. We hired a marquee, an extra fridge, and bought wine online.

I asked my youngest son to walk me down the aisle and Heather asked one of her brothers. I asked if my two-year-old twin granddaughters could be flower girls and my older granddaughters to be part of the wedding party. My best friend offered to be my legs, as I was still in plaster, and to do all the fetching and carrying. My New Zealand friends were asked to be part of the ritual and read the invocation I wrote.

Hail Guardians of the East
I summon the powers of the Air
By the air that is Her breath
Be with us now!

Hail Guardians of the South
I summon the powers of Fire
By the fire that is Her spirit
Be with us now!

Hail Guardians of the West
I summon the powers of Water
By the water of Her womb
Be with us now!

Hail Guardians of the North
We summon the powers of the Earth
By the Earth that is Her body
Be with us now!

Our Commitment Ceremony

As above, so below
As within, so without
Woven together
To make the circle complete!

So Mote It Be
In Perfect Love and Perfect
Trust, Blessed Be.

Ritual words similar to these have been spoken by women down through the ages. While I write I can picture in my mind those women, standing barefoot on grassy hilltops with the moon riding high in the sky, or under the cloak of darkness when the moon is a thin white sickle drawn in velvet. Women have sung words such as these whenever the Goddess has been invoked by one of Her many names. I wrote these words to invite the four directions, the four Goddesses, to join us on our special day.

Heather wants to hold our ceremony at her family home for two reasons: this would be the last formal family gathering before the property is put on the market, and both her sisters held their weddings under the magnificent Jacaranda tree that dominates the back garden.

Late in the afternoon, we call for a circle to be formed. Our marriage celebrant is in a magnificent flowing robe, family and friends in informal dress, my grandchildren wearing special dresses for their grandmother's 'wedding'. A hush descends as the ritual begins. There is a ripple of surprise from those who might have been expecting something more Catholic and less Pagan. After the calling of the four directions, candles are lit for those elders not present, and for family and friends unable to attend. I'm helped to my feet from the chair where I've been sitting, my plastered leg hidden beneath my linen trousers. Heather and I have written our vows, promises to each other of lasting love and friendship until the end of our days.

As a sprinkling of happy tears falls from the sky, we retire to the marquee to share a meal, to drink sparkling wine and to cut our special cake. All the while, the grandchildren are running around showing off their special fancy dresses with their wide sash bows, friends and family are introducing themselves and the photographer is snapping happy pics to later be made into an album.

There is no honeymoon, no weekend away, it is back to work the next day but with the biggest smiles on our faces and new sparkling jewels on our ring fingers.

Many Years Later, the marriage celebrant will pass the microphone to Heather who will read:

"The occasion of Marriage Equality and this particular day came at great personal expense to me, to Hannah and to many, many LGBTQI Australians.

"To the uninitiated, it was a simple Postal Survey, no more, no less. What's all the fuss about? I'm all for it, sure, vote yes and move on.

"We want to thank all of you for your support, and here I must say we assume each of you voted YES - why else would you be here to celebrate with us?

"During the weeks-long agony between the survey being distributed and the results being announced, we, the people who were being impacted, heard our lives being openly discussed in pubs, on public transport, walking down the street, in cafes and in parks like this one. (Sydney Park) Mentioned as casually as choosing between ice-cream or cream, it wasn't about *real people* and certainly not the real people sitting right next to you.

"Those discussions were had by people who believed WE have no right to be treated as an equal citizen of this country. We endured the snipes about our children and how they would be better off in 'normal families', whatever that means. How the world would end if we were allowed to marry. How this was the slippery slope to debauchery. There were threats, there was violence and there was disgusting graffiti all over the country.

"I cannot describe how deeply it affected me. It hit like a bolt from the blue, so unexpected, so heavy and so complete. With Hannah's help, I had the sense to seek out a counsellor to help me get through it and my Tuesday visits to Andrew saved my life and my sanity. I know, with sadness, that others were not so fortunate.

"On the day of the results, Hannah and I and our friends were in Prince Alfred Park for the announcement and it was an agonising wait. When the numbers were read out by the Head Statistician we, all of us there, heard nothing else, until finally, he said YES 61.6%... NO 38.4%.

"WE HAD WON! It was such a relief to hear those numbers... WE HAD WON! It felt like we had been holding our breath for all those weeks and finally, we could breathe again. But there was sadness, too, knowing that 38% still don't believe Hannah and I should be treated just like them, that we are in some way abnormal, different.

"Today we choose to embrace that difference and rub the noses of the 38% in the dirt as we take the tradition of Marriage as our own.

"Thank you all for helping us celebrate a day we never thought possible."

6

Being A Dog Groomer

I didn't know that when Heather left the house each morning it was with a sense of dread. I thought the four-week grooming course had set her up to be a competent dog groomer and she was going off to work with confidence, having begun her new career. But that wasn't how she felt and wasn't what was happening for her as she pulled away each day from the house and drove to her first client of the day.

In reality, she was living under the enormous pressure of pleasing clients who were used to paying for a professional groom from an experienced groomer, and Heather knew the four-week course had given her little more than the most basic and rudimentary skills.

She didn't talk about how she was feeling, how alone she felt, after the support and camaraderie of her tutor and classmates. Now she was totally alone with only her training manuals and large ring binder pictorial instructions of breed clips for help. She needed the business to succeed, to keep money coming in, plus meet the exacting requirements of fussy dog owners.

I was too busy, too happy, too engrossed in my own world to notice how quiet and shutdown she had become. While I was elated and pleased with all I was learning, enjoying trying new things, Heather was locked into feeling the opposite. I had always been told I was stupid, dumb and lacked the ability to learn or succeed. Heather, on the other hand, for thirty years had steadily risen through the ranks of a male-dominated industry where women needed to show twice the skill and aptitude to be given half the advancement. It had been many years since she was a beginner, learning and developing new skills, being an apprentice rather than an accomplished master.

She was also struggling with her years of being a depot supervisor in an organisation that didn't allow middle management to make decisions or demands because there was always someone on the leader rung above. Heather might have a hundred workers under her control, but she was never in a position to make suggestions, to change rules or step outside her narrow role definition. Her job was to be a loyal employee, to comply with company rules, to manage the day to day running of the depot and ensure the buses and drivers followed the schedule so the depot ticked over with routine effectiveness and efficiency. She was not encouraged or expected to speak out of turn.

Adding to this feeling of isolation was the unspoken division of labour with all things dog grooming falling under Heather's jurisdiction, while the rest of the business became my project while my leg was in plaster. Heather was in charge of making the dog grooming appointments, invoicing and subsequent payments. Ordering grooming supplies, the tubs of shampoo, the sharpening of blades, keeping the van in good mechanical order. She had little need for a desk at home as most of her dealings with her clients took place in the van. She threw her appointment book, receipt book, and various order and delivery dockets onto the van dashboard, along with pens and pencils, spare dog collars, a broken handset and spare boxes of clipper blades. If this was her new office, the back was her new salon.

The Grooming Van

The fit-out in the back of the van was designed for maximum space for the groomer to move around, while cramming in all the essentials to groom dogs, the large plastic washtub against the wall behind the driver's seat. It had a long shelf for the pump-action tubs of shampoos and conditioners, the shelf to the left holding all the neatly folded towels. The three-speed power drier was next and then you could step out of the back doors. On the other side, after the sliding door was the adjustable grooming table with a set of plastic drawers attached to the van body at head height, for the hand clippers, boxes of blades, and the dozens of pairs of scissors and shears, straight blades, curved blades and hair thinners with tiny metal teeth. The reels for a water hose and power cord were mounted in the middle on the back wall separating the front driving cabin from the back.

"What are you doing?"

"Writing about the grooming van," I say, as Heather comes in from hanging out the washing. "I'm describing the back of the van and how compact it was in design while still being a very tight space to work in."

"Tell me about it," she says, resting both arms on the back of my chair and reading over my shoulder.

Heather read out my words, "It was boiling hot in summer even with the van being painted white, and freezing in winter because there was no insulation. I'd have all the doors open in the heat, the side sliding door and the two back doors, and then have to shut them when it was windy or wet or cold and I'd feel like I was shut in a fridge."

I wait for her to go on. "At the end of the day my legs would be aching, my back hurt, I usually had a splitting headache from worrying so much. I knew I wasn't doing a good job; I was scared someone was going to yell at me and refuse to pay. I got blisters from the damn grooming scissors, I don't know how many times I burnt myself on the hot grooming blades, and remember those little festering 'things' I got in my fingers from the hair splinters. You got quite good with a needle popping them."

She comes around, sits in her office chair beside me and recalls, "I got to the stage where I hated it, the grooming, dog owners who either couldn't care for their dogs or didn't realise how much attention dogs need. The ones who didn't even brush their dog from the month I saw them until the month when I came back. The poor dog with knots in its armpits, around its collar, down its back legs. I'd be the bad groomer pulling out the knots, trying to ease out the tangles, and then half the time the only thing to do was shave the poor thing off clean." She settles back in the chair, frowning, arms folded.

"There were times when I was close to tears with the condition of some dogs. I remember an old dog with so many fleas I wanted to call the RSPCA. By the time I'd finished washing him *the water was black*."

"Why didn't you?" I ask. "Call the authorities?"

"And what would they do? They could tell the old girl off, take the dog, and then what?"

"Why didn't you talk to me about what was happening, about how you felt, about the dogs, how horrible some of the owners were?" I'm also sitting back now, the writing forgotten. I feel we might finally be able to talk about that time, a time when we were both working so hard but separate and not relating well with each other.

"It was hard, physical work. I'd spent years in an office or driving around in a van checking buses were turning up on the route, on time. Then it was one thing after another; we started living together, mum died, the accident with my eye and the constant operations and appointments at the hospital, then we bought the business, the commitment ceremony."

"I remember us talking on the phone before I came over, about how you might feel when your mother died. I know I was so angry when my mother had her stroke and she lost the ability to speak. I felt we were just starting to talk, have a real conversation, get somewhere, maybe finally know each other."

"Mum was in her nineties and ready to go. Dad had died so young and I missed him terribly, and it was hard losing mum. You think your parents are going to be around forever." She reaches over for my hand. "I'm glad you got to meet her while she was alive, even if it was from her hospital bed."

I let the silence take over before asking. "How difficult were those years?"

It's hard to listen to, Heather tells it like a story about someone else's life, but I know there's pain hidden beneath her words.

In Business Together

"The clients didn't understand the difference between taking their dog to a salon and having me come to their house. I had to set the van up at every place, get the van off the road, get it level so I could have the dog stand on the grooming table, attach the hose for the washtub to their garden tap, run the power cable up to the house and through the front bedroom window or maybe the garage."

"Get the dog, put him in the tub, wash and dry, do the groom, put the dog back in the yard or the house, clean out the van, get rid of the dog hair, roll up the hose and power cord, make the next booking, take the money, drive on to the next address." She pauses. "It doesn't sound that hard or take that long when you're sitting in a comfortable chair prattling on."

"However, I was on my own, just one person, whereas at the main street salon they were all set up and had junior staff doing the washing, blow-dry and comb-outs, ready for the groomer."

"That's all the groomer had to do all day; groom a perfectly washed and dried dog ready for clipping and if the dog got snappy or tired the junior would put it in the playpen and the groomer would carry on with another dog. I'd have to work with one dog, from beginning to end, and it would take hours and hours, especially when I was just a beginner. Working in the van was noisy, the washtub, then the blow drier and the continual buzzing of the clippers. The van rocked when the heavy trucks trundled past, and that frightened some of the dogs."

"I'd have the bloody owner bouncing around at the back of the van, making sure I didn't hurt her 'baby', the dog wouldn't do what I wanted, it only wanted to look at the owner. Or I'd be working away, and some random passer-by would pop their head through the door and give me a fright; either I'd cut a chunk of hair out of the dog or it would try to leap off the table."

I can't help myself, I giggle.

"It's not funny, one wrong move with the clippers and you had a bald dog!"

I know I shouldn't laugh but Heather's face as she's telling the story is all red and cross and I can't help but be amused. It's sad really, I had no idea for years that she felt this way or was struggling. After my leg was out of plaster and I was able to go back to walking dogs we didn't talk about the dog grooming part of the business, but we could have just stopped. Heather and I could have both walked dogs and done the pet sitting. It would have been more practical and earned more money.

But we weren't talking, we weren't having 'business meetings' where we discussed what was happening in the business. We were so focused on working hard, we weren't thinking like business owners and planning how we wanted to grow the business and what direction we wanted it to take.

"Of course," says Heather quietly, "the big problem was my sight."

This was something else Heather hadn't talked about. I assumed, wrongly, that her sight was like mine if I closed one eye, but it wasn't. The cornea had been ripped when the glass flew into the eyeball and when Heather pulled the glass out the eyeball had deflated, leaking out the fluid. In the initial surgery, they had repaired the damage with stitches and reinflated the eye. But the damage wasn't a straight cut, it was jagged, and the damaged eye no longer reacted to the light and dark. There was fuzzy shading if Heather closed her good eye and looked with only her damaged eye. She might be able to see I was wearing something blue but not be able to tell if it was a jumper or a tee-shirt. She might know someone was approaching but not able to see their features and know who they were. She also had problems with her depth vision, so parts of the groomed fur might be longer than other parts.

The problem in the van was the harsh direct sunlight that her damaged retina couldn't adjust to, which caused her sight to be disturbed while at the same time not having enough direct light on the areas she was trying to trim. She was either blinded by sunlight bouncing around the white interior of the van or unable to see in the dim light. Even with several spotlights, she was still struggling with her depth perception, often trimming two sections of the fur to different lengths. With no peripheral vision in the damaged eye, she was forever banging and scraping her head, elbow or knee and often when pouring her tea would just miss the cup by a hair's breadth.

"But that wasn't your major belly-ache when you were first out grooming. I seem to remember night after night your whining about not having enough time in the day for lunch or a hot drink."

Now it's Heather's turn to giggle. "I know, it seems ridiculous now, but at the time I just didn't get it."

Every night it was the same. Heather would storm into the house, drop her bag on the floor, and start opening and closing cupboard doors as she made a sandwich and hot drink. She'd complain about not having a break, never having time to go to the toilet, eat lunch or grab a coffee.

"Well," I'd say, "Talk to the boss and get him to change your work schedule." I was being a smarty pants and not taking her complaints seriously, sitting back watching her let off steam. It was the same night after night for weeks, until I'd finally had enough of the uproar and noise.

"You know you're the one that books your client's grooms, and organises your daily schedule, don't you." I try to keep my mother's sarcasm out of my voice.

"I'm doing what the client wants, booking the time they ask, squeezing as many dogs in as I can. It's not easy. I'm slow, much slower than they're used to, and they think I should be able to keep up the same schedule as they've been used to over the last six years."

"Why should you have to do it the same way? Why don't you just tell them you're only learning, and you'll get faster." I'm trying to think of ways I can help. "I'll send out a newsletter and explain you can only book half the number each day and so the clients that were having their dog groomed every four weeks will have to wait for six and the six-week grooms will be every second month." Heather looks terrified at this suggestion.

"You can't do that, there'll be complaints, nasty phone calls, letters, I'll lose my job."

"You're kidding aren't you?" But one look at her face tells me she's not understanding my point. "You are the boss, you own the business, you get to make the decisions, you're the person who gets the complaints, the nasty phone calls, the letters. You're it, sweetheart, the buck stops right here!"

She looks stunned, as if I'd just hit her in the face with a wet fish. "You-are-the-boss. Make the day work for *you*, talk to the clients, explain and the ones that don't stay, well, that's their choice, we'll find new ones."

I move to sit closer, I take her hand. "You're not working in some male-dominated industry now. It's just you and me, running a little dog service business from our home, from our living room, from a computer and desk. We have to figure it out, we have to learn how to manage, how to be the boss and the workers, how to earn enough money but also to be happy, to enjoy what we do."

"It's so hard," says Heather. "I don't know what I'm doing half the time and I keep making mistakes. I'm so slow and when I hurry I forget things, I didn't clip Harry's nails and poor Flin didn't get his treat, I just bundled him out of the van because I was running late for Joan, and she always complains."

It all comes pouring out, the months of pent-up emotion, the worry about being a groomer, her fears about losing the house, the self-hate and putting herself down. A long list of self-imposed inadequacies, her inexperience, being unable to talk about it, fear of disappointing me, letting me down, not living up to my expectations, not being good enough.

It's like a wall crumbles and suddenly we're able to talk, *really* talk. Just how frightening and scary it is having total responsibility for every aspect of your life, home, work, a relationship, a business. There's no part of it where you can blame someone else, take a break, let it all go for a week. It's twenty-four-seven, relentless, ticking away in your mind, always alert to the phone ringing, the next client booking. There's no ducking for cover, staying in bed and pulling the covers over your head, taking a sick day when it suits you. It's on you, every day. That's the reality of running your own business.

"Let's have a cup of tea and then I need to check that invoice for Marion; she wants to add a day to her pet sit next week." And just like that, we break apart and I head for my desk and Heather puts the kettle on.

7

We Make A Plan

"It's out of control, the business. It's out of control."

We're at the breakfast table. From where I'm sitting I can see through the window the new wooden fence. We've only been back in the house, after the renovations, for three months. We'd stayed with friends while the nearly hundred-year-old terrace was gutted, five fireplaces and three chimneys were removed. The old washhouse and toilet had been demolished and moved inside. The new bathroom with a walk-in shower and overhead rain head was a thing of beauty. The other indulgence was the new concrete polished floor with underfloor heating. We had our desks moved to the new open living area at the back of the house because the wall of glass sliding doors let in so much more light.

"What do you mean 'out of control'?" asks Heather.

In my head, I see the business as a galloping horse racing ahead in the distance, and no matter how hard I try, I can't catch it. Every day I know I'm falling further and further behind, no matter how much time I spend working, there's always more to do. Since I've had the plaster removed from my broken ankle and was back on my feet, I've been walking dogs five days a week. Heather and I share the pet sitting but I'm left to keep up with answering emails, admin and social media. The business has been growing at a steady rate with a mix of word-of-mouth and social media. We've taken on new clients and while that's great, I'm not getting ahead, and everything feels out of control.

I'm tired and grumpy, I'm not sleeping properly, tossing and turning, with everything that has to be done whirring around in my head. I've been getting up earlier and earlier, trying to catch up, but I know this can't go on. I'm resentful and angry toward Heather. She comes home in the afternoon, makes a hot drink and puts her feet up on the couch. She's on her bum while I'm still thumbing away on the computer.

My physical day starts at nine, picking up dogs in groups of four and spending an hour in the dog park with them. I return them to their homes and collect the next group. I finish the third and last walk, making it home before five. At my desk I begin answering emails, making bookings, talking to new clients, scheduling Meet and Greet appointments and arranging the pickup of house keys. We'd come so far since the early days with scraps of paper with hand-written notes in old boxes.

Clients' personal and pet details are recorded in the database and again in the newsletter list. It's time-consuming and double handling but with no idea the business would grow so quickly, I'd chosen the most basic options when selecting marketing platforms.

With the business doubling and in some areas, tripling, not only had it grown beyond my control, but it had outgrown the systems I'd put in place. Every aspect of the business structure and day to day running needed to be overhauled, updated and improved.

"I'm not coping," I say, holding back the tears. "It doesn't matter how late I stay up or how early I get up, there's always more to do than I can manage." I can feel the anger jammed up in the back of my throat. "And there's housework, grocery shopping and an afternoon off wouldn't go amiss." I know I'm bleating on, but I feel I have no control over my life.

"What are you talking about?" says Heather. "Everything's fine. I've got my speed up and I'm doing three grooms and on a good day, an added wash. I know all the client's addresses, the name of their dogs, what type of groom they want and I'm rebooking them every six weeks." She rattles this off, waving her toast around in the air as she talks.

"Most have the correct cash and I've told Louise I'm not taking any more cheques. I've had a talk with the son of that old lady on Woodlands Street and told him to tell her to stop washing the dog in dishwashing liquid and it wouldn't have any skin issues." Heather ticks off her accomplishments.

I watch Heather's mouth as it opens and closes, her words flowing around me. Nothing she's saying matches what's happening for me. She's talking about another business, as if what she does in the grooming van each day has nothing to do with the hours I spend on the computer.

And I realise we *are* talking about different businesses. Heather's talking about a mobile dog grooming business she manages and has under control.

I'm talking about a dog walking and pet sitting business I'm not managing, and which is out of control.

"I'm talking about all the admin, the paperwork, the very heart of our business. You're talking about one arm of the business. The same as the dog walking is 'one arm' and the pet sitting is 'one arm'. We can't run an effective business from only the 'arms' we are responsible for. We have to manage the business from the heart."

It all begins to make sense. I see this out-of-control octopus with three ever-growing, longer arms. It began with that box of client records, handwritten on sheets of paper when I was laid up with my broken ankle. I'd simply sought an affordable, preferably free, platform and transferred the client names and personal and pet details into the program. Everything was very basic, because at the time I had no computer experience, but that had changed over the last few years.

Heather had managed the grooming van and when I was back on my feet I'd walked dogs and done the pet sitting. It was a fair and logical sharing of the physical work. What hadn't evolved with the growth of the business was an effective business structure. We had split the workload and in doing so had halved the business. I wasn't sure we could genuinely be called business partners right now. I was beginning to think we were two friends running similar pet service businesses from the same address.

"You know we can't go on like this," I say. "We can't treat the business as if the two halves don't belong to the same business. And we've got to start dealing with this as business partners. You can't just say what you're doing is working okay and I should get on with what I'm doing."

I'm shocked by how much we have drifted apart. How much distance there is between us. We seem to have lost touch with each other. It begins to make sense why we don't talk anymore, why we aren't intimate or spending time together. We've become strangers with no idea of what each other needs.

"Don't you see; we've stopped being *partners*," I'm pleading my case, trying to make Heather understand what I see. "Everything has been piling up on top of us and we're only seeing our own little bit of the business. We have no big picture, no plan. We're letting the business run us, not us running the business. We're just getting up and going to work, on automatic, as if you still work on the buses for State Transit or I managed that bloody awful bedding and towel shop."

I go back to staring out the window at the fence. In my head I can hear all those judgemental voices 'You're too old', 'What a nice hobby for two friends', 'A little top-up to help with the pension', 'You should leave it to the younger ones and stop making fools of yourselves.'

We don't need to listen to other people's summations and negativity about our ability to run our own business; we've been doing a perfectly good job at doubting ourselves.

I get up from the table and go to my desk. "If we're going to stop acting like amateurs and treating this business as a hobby, we need to get organised, rethink everything, get it together, make a plan."

Heather begins to laugh. "Of course we need a plan; let's make a plan, get out your pad and pen and we'll make a list and then make a plan." She grins, teasing.

It feels good to be made fun of and I smile back in relief. It feels like the first normal thing we've done together in so long. It feels like I'm back on solid ground after standing alone overlooking a precipice.

"This is serious," I say, returning to my seat. "We've got to get serious. We've hardly talked about the business since the renovations. It was alright to let things tick over while we weren't living in the house but that's over and we have to take responsibility and make decisions about what it is we want from being in business, how big do we want the business to be?"

I move the plates aside for the pad and divide the page in half by drawing a line down the middle. "Pour another cup of tea and let's make a plan."

The Plan

This was a typical spontaneous business meeting. We've tried scheduling meetings once a week after dinner, but we were always too tired. Breakfast meetings seemed like a good idea, too, but the cafes were too noisy. We tried monthly meetings but somehow they always got pushed back when something came up.

It was a bit like our 'date' night. Even if we could agree on what to do and where to go, we often cancelled because we were too tired to make the effort to change out of our uniform and leave the house. And when we did leave the house, we still talked business. We'd been so preoccupied with the business we hadn't taken the time to develop a separate social life. We had become friendly with some of our clients, but those acquaintanceships didn't give us the personal or business support we needed.

"Business plan, what's first?" We sit in silence, not looking at each other, thinking, trying to pick up the conversation. "Okay, let's break it down," I say, in an effort to get started. "We'll do a mind map 'thingy' and just scribble down ideas and see what comes up." Heather looks sceptical as I draw several large circles on the page.

This is my creative method for working through problems. Whether it's a Facebook post, a newsletter, a blog or a book, I start by letting random thoughts and ideas flow onto the page.

"First," I say, "we need to let go of the fears we had when we bought the business, like losing the house or not being able to make a go of it - look, we're halfway through the fourth year and not living on the streets. And I need to stop feeling guilty that I pushed you into buying the business. I've always worried that I didn't put money in to buy the business and you did."

"About time; I couldn't have done this on my own," says Heather. "I don't know what I'd have been doing now but it wouldn't have been dog grooming."

"The business has become bigger than the two of us can manage. We need to hire a dog walker."

I don't know why we'd never talked about how big we wanted the business to grow; did we want to keep it to just us or have other people involved? It was as if by talking about the size and direction of the business we were 'jinxing' ourselves. As if we never talked out loud, things would be alright, when in reality the opposite was true. If we'd had a business plan, had talked about our hopes and dreams for the business often, we'd be in better shape right now. We'd been so busy working *in* the business we hadn't taken the time to work *on* the business. It was time to look up and forward to making a plan, so we knew where we wanted to go. Instead of following, we needed to be leading.

"How are the clients going to feel about that; it's always been just us." Heather's point brings up another aspect we've never given thought to. We've made the business all about us. Our photos on the webpage and social media. We've been hands-on, talking with every client, learning about each dog, every pet. The idea of bringing in a stranger hasn't ever been mentioned.

"You don't want someone to run the office?"

"No," I say. "I love writing the newsletter, posting on Facebook and I'm happy to be at home working on the computer."

"You mean not having to meet or talk to anyone. Staying at home and making sure the washing doesn't get wet." Heather's smiling as she points her finger knowingly at me. "Where are we going to find a dog walker?"

"I'll put an ad in the paper and when I'm in the park today I'll let the other dog walkers know we're looking for staff. If we put it out there, someone will pop up." I feel buoyed up by the idea of getting some help.

"What else?" asks Heather, peering at my scribbled list.

"I signed us up on Mailchimp when we first started, it was low cost and under the paid prescription rate, but what I'm reading is that we need a full CRM." Heather looks uncertain. "A Customer Relationship Management 'thingy'," I say. "It will allow us to gather more useful data, target the individual services, send out birthday emails, announce upcoming specials."

Most of my business knowledge has come from reading and surfing business articles, blogs and newsletters. I've found women's business pages on Facebook and in the years I've been following the most helpful ones, I've joined free courses, challenges, anything I feel will increase my knowledge and understanding about how to run a home-based business. I'm a lurker, reading the questions and a wide variety of answers. I've tried ideas from my diverse reading and slowly figured out what works for us and what doesn't.

"You know what would be really helpful," says Heather, twisting the pad round and taking the pen. "A booking system specifically designed for dog grooming, dog walking and pet sitting. She's drawing a chart with arrows of how the database would connect the client to us. "A database for all the personal and pet information of the client. A way for the client to book or cancel their service, charge or update information, be invoiced and have their credit card details held for quick online payment."

"It would certainly cut down my work." I can envisage three and four time-consuming manual admin jobs being condensed into one software program. While the idea is exciting, I'm wondering about the cost of moving to high tech programs.

"I'll contact the Pets Industry Association," I suggest. "They might have some information. I could try Google and ask the other dog walkers what software they use."

I have a list of To-Do items and a bit of a plan. I'll start gathering information. I feel as if we've taken the business 'to the next level'. It's a catchphrase used by online business coaches, those women who look like 'real' businesswomen dressed in office clothing, sitting behind a desk, decorated tastefully with a neat pile of books and a vase of flowers. In contrast, I feel scruffy and dressed down in my printed tee-shirt, work pants and running shoes. Now I feel a bit more like a businesswoman looking for staff, a super-duper CRM and professional pet industry software.

"And we need to start networking," I state, turning to a new page. "We can't keep working in a vacuum, not knowing what other businesses are doing, trying to figure out everything for ourselves. We need to be working with other businesspeople, talking to other businesses, showing we're locals."

"What's sparked this off?"

"The council," I say. "They are starting a small business group initiative and we've been invited."

Networking

I have a love-hate relationship with networking. I enjoy talking one on one with an interesting woman about what she is doing in her business, what she's passionate about, her creativity, and ambitions. I don't like sitting in a room of strangers, managing a glass of something in one hand, a rice-paper nibble in the other, and chatting. It's tedious and as my eyes glaze over, I begin to think of how many words I could have written.

What I did find useful was a small, local council-run group, held at a local business premises, monthly. There was a committed core group who turned up for the coffee and tea and we sat around and talked about a specific topic. Most months one business owner would take the lead and talk about his or her business specifics, offering ideas, support and further information. From this group, we'd used the services of a photographer, printer and bookkeeper. It was a friendly, open group who didn't have any of the time-consuming issues of organisation, because the council saw to that.

"I'm going to start a women's home-based business group," I announced six months later, as we were clearing away dinner. "I think women work differently to men and I'm sick of having men hijack the floor when we're talking in the group."

When I'd first started going to the monthly business meetings I was still trying to feel as if I fitted in. The group seemed to be made up of the professional class, lawyers, bookkeepers and accountants, real estate agents, the CEO of a distribution company, medical professionals, IT companies. I'd felt a bit intimidated, as if I and my little dog walking business didn't belong. But over time I'd realised that, big or small, we were all facing the same problems; trying to make money, find clients or customers, trying to sell our products and services. The big difference for me was the attitudes between the men and women. I found women and men had different business ethics and values, different leadership styles, and different attitudes and ideas about the use of power. I believed women wanted to work from a position of compassion and empathy, and were more inclined to be cooperative than aggressive.

"Is this like the time you organised a class to learn astrology because the teacher didn't work one on one?" asks Heather.

She's talking about my wanting to learn astrology, where I had to organise a group of fifteen women over a ten-week course before the teacher would entertain the idea. I wasn't afraid to be an organiser, a planner. I'd read once it was a trait of an alcoholic. For the book launches I'd organised, for my collections of poetry and short story work, I usually organised other artists to join me. The biggest event I had put together was with three other artists, a photographer who specialised in portraiture, a sculptor who produced exquisite eighteen inch tall sandstone figurines, and a local newly-formed woman's rock band. It was the only way I could get the paper interested in covering the group and being able to pay the cost of hiring a wonderful setting for the evening.

"Well, my need right now is a group of women who work from home and understand the difficulties of having to be self-motivated. I want to be talking to women who want to change the way they do business from the masculine to the feminine, from overpower to soft power. The change in business today is around values, people culture, and earth-friendly."

Within six months we were meeting at a local restaurant once a month, having drinks, dinner and a free-for-all discussion on whatever topic was brought up. Some women used the gatherings as purely social events and others were able to talk through issues they were encountering in their business. I wasn't the only one working with an intimate and business partner and it made for some funny stories.

Being Women

"I'm writing about the times we were treated differently because we were women in business," I say, swinging round in my office chair. "Care to give me your thoughts?"

"My brothers were sceptical," says Heather. "And do you remember that accountant who never sent us an invoice for a whole year?"

Heather called him up after reading his ad in the local paper. Yes, there was a time when we still read and took note of the local paper, not now; the internet has taken over. Anyway, this local accountant was offering a free consultation to new businesses and Heather made an appointment and went to his office.

He seemed like a nice guy, big smile, happy to help us get started. He suggested MYOB and set up our accounts, we use Xero now. He recommended several local bookkeepers when Heather confessed that neither of us has a head for figures. We both attended several meetings over the first twelve months, and he'd nod and smile and say we were doing well and set our next target. We never got a bill. When we asked about an account in the second year he sat forward in his chair, elbows propped on his desk and said frankly, "I didn't think you were going to survive in your business. I thought you were too old, you had no business experience and while you loved dogs, I didn't think you'd be able to manage the physical work of handling them. I liked you both. I loved your enthusiasm and commitment but on paper, I just didn't see it working." He smiled apologetically.

And he wasn't the only one. Apparently, some of the professional dog walkers who saw us turning up day after day in the dog park also didn't see our business lasting, they took us for too old. Heather's family struggled to understand why we couldn't just drive up the Coast to join them for Christmas dinner. It was only some new folly Heather and her new girlfriend were doing and surely we could walk away to be with family? The argument raged on for several years until they finally realised that, not only was the new girlfriend going to stay, so was our commitment to our business.

At our women's group, not being supported by a partner, friends or family was a painfully familiar talking point. It seemed a man starting a business and working long hours and earning little in the first start-up years was seen as commendable, whereas in a woman it was selfish. While I was happy to be a dog walker and weekend carer of pets, there were women who wanted to become business leaders in their field, wanted to be entrepreneurs, business influencers, build a business that had turnovers in the millions, yet who suffered from a lack of self-confidence because of what people were saying about them and to them.

There were times in our business when our services were not seen or treated as professional. When we weren't treated as professionals but as uniformed hired help that could be talked down to or treated as a lower class. Women who talked down to me set off my shame triggers; I felt belittled, dirty, as if when I left their home I needed a shower. We didn't book repeat business with these clients.

In saying this I'm willing to acknowledge it took time to present ourselves as professionals. We did, in the beginning, feel like imposters, as if what we did had little value and we felt uncomfortable asking for payment. As we began to value ourselves and the services we provided, our self-esteem grew, and we perfected our 'elevator pitch'.

We also began to take control of the Meet and Greets with new clients. At first, being in someone's home, we expected they would lead the conversation about what they needed from us and our service. We began to recognise the new client often needed us to direct the discussion and to that end, we drew up a list of questions on a clipboard to ask.

Being our age and being female was a definite advantage, we realised, when dealing with pet owners who were women. Women felt more relaxed and safer handing over their house keys to us when they were going on holiday and we were caring for their pet, or picking up their pup to walk. We were seen as 'mums' to their dog or cat, a second parent and that worked in our favour. At our age, we were viewed as reliable, trustworthy, sensible, and seen as efficient cleaners at keeping pet feeding and toilet areas tidy.

Being Lesbian

Heather and I have never hidden the fact we were gay, in fact, in the beginning, we traded on it. We bought the mobile grooming van from a gay man and our first prejudiced reactions were actually from gay clients who didn't want to deal with lesbians. There's a historical background to this that I won't go into here, but being gay doesn't automatically mean empathy with every segment of the gay community. There were some lovely old 'Queens' who welcomed Heather with joy and some unpleasant younger men we were happy to strike off our books.

When we began planning an update to the webpage we inherited with the sale of the business, we made sure to put both our photos at the head of the pages and to talk openly about being 'life partners'- of course now we're able to use the word 'wives'. Again we came under fire for 'having to push our agenda'. I have always been 'Out', the term used when you don't hide your sexuality. As a feminist lesbian, my being honest and upfront about my true self is less about who I prefer to sleep with and more about my political commitment to and emotional attachment with women.

We did, understandably, gain a large number of lesbian and gay clients. Everyone feels more comfortable with others who understand them, and they don't have to explain themselves. In those early years when we did a customer profile, our typical client was female, 30 to 45 years old, gay, split 50/50 single or partner, childless, renter, inner-city apartment or share-house, middle income, career-oriented, white. In the last years of our business our clients were both male and female, 38 to 56 years, gay or heterosexual, married or partnered, 1-3 children, homeowners, double income, long term career prospects, white.

"Have you finished that chapter yet?" Heather calls from the kitchen. "Dinner is on the table."

8

We Need Dog Walkers

"So, you want to walk dogs?"

"Yes, I love dogs. How much is the pay?"

Wrong answer. I'm looking for 'Walking dogs would be the best job in the world' or 'We had a little dog when I was a kid' or 'The neighbour, grandma, a friend, had a little white fluffy that I walked after school' or 'I'm enrolled in Animal Studies at TAFE and want to work in the industry.' Being passionate about dogs is essential, everything else can be taught.

The advertised position for a Dog Walker came with a list of requirements:
- Own car, suitable for dogs
- Clean driving record
- Police clearance
- Two referees
- Smartphone (We have computer software with an app for dog walkers)

In Business Together

- Live in the area or know the surrounding suburbs
- We have to like you

We'd start with a quick chat over the phone and if we liked the way the conversation was going arrange a face to face interview at the house. The house was our home and our office. Another intertwined aspect of our personal and business lives. There was no clear line between us, the people who lived in the home, and us, the business owners, managing employees from the living area of our house. Owning and managing a home-based business meant having our employees coming in and out of our home every day. We had to create an atmosphere of business, regardless of the smell of our breakfast bacon and eggs hanging in the air. We had no dark panelled door with our name and title on, no large desk to sit behind, no power suits. For us, the dog walking team gathered around the kitchen table, and it immediately meant having a different relationship with them, more intimate and no ability to hide behind the formal trappings of being the boss.

If a prospective dog walker was given an interview time but turned up late without phoning or texting that was interpreted as not taking the position seriously, they weren't reliable, or they were unable to follow basic instructions. For any of these reasons, they wouldn't be hired. We were looking for reliability, being practical and able to think on their feet and problem solve. We didn't have time to jump in the car and rush to a client's house because a dog walker couldn't get the key to work. We did, however, encourage phone calls and had a list of questions ready:

- Are you at the correct address?
- Using the correct key, front screen door, front door, back door, yard gate?
- Correct apartment block?

- Correct lift, correct floor?
- Have you tried jiggling the key?
- Does the door need to be lifted slightly?
- Have you tried shoving the door with your knee, hip, full-body blow?

While all of the above was covered in the training period, where the new dog walker would ride along and shadow us, we knew that first time on their own could be daunting. Every new dog walker chose the day they were ready to go out on their own. Some people were confident and knew the suburbs within one to two weeks, while others took longer. Each new dog walker was told, "I don't care how often you ask a question, but the first time you messed up is because you didn't ask."

A dog walker's first responsibility was their safety and the safety of the client's dog. This meant the dog didn't get hurt, wasn't in a fight, wasn't lost, and had a great time playing in the dog park. To ensure the dog walker was doing their job and to show the client how much fun their pup was having, the walkers did a Facebook live video, plus still shots. We didn't allow photos of dogs fighting, showing their teeth, humping, toileting, or behaving in any way that could be misconstrued by an owner sitting at their office desk. These live broadcasts and pics were eagerly awaited by owners and I often received calls saying, 'I haven't seen George on his walk yet.'

One of the main reasons our services were engaged and why we posted videos and photos of the dog walks, was to reduce the guilt owners felt at leaving their pet at home for eight to ten hours each day. The majority of owners walked their dogs before or after work or both. We didn't take the dog out purely for exercise; our mission was to pick up the dog and give it an hour of socialisation, fun and play with other dogs. We would break up the dog's day, toilet it outside, and enjoy some interactive stimulation. Dogs need regular social interaction for their health and mental wellbeing.

Over our ten years in the pet business, we've had some amazing people work with us. They've all been different ages, sizes, religions, from different countries. There's no one personality type; we've had the loudest, most outgoing people who blow through the house every morning and afternoon like a comedy show, and others who were so quiet even the dogs didn't react. But the common thread was their love and commitment to the dogs they handled daily.

"Remember that woman," Heather says, "who turned up wanting to work with dogs but not pick up dog poo?"

Picking up dog poo is the bane of a dog walker's life. You end up not only picking up after your own dogs but also picking up after any dog. It's a health issue; dog poo is toxic and carries bacteria, but how I always like to explain it is that the dog park is like our office; we're there five days a week, from ten in the morning until four in the afternoon, and have a responsibility to keep it clean. I don't care if the dog poo isn't from the dogs we are walking, all dog poo needs to be picked up and put in the rubbish bins provided.

"How much dog poo do you think we've picked up over the last ten years?" I ask, thinking of all the videos that show me in the background of a dog walk, bent over and picking the stuff up. "In the hour we spend in the park, on average I'd fill three to four of those black poo bags." The rolls of poo bags were put out by the council next to the council rubbish bins in every dog park. For the first few years of the business we were reliant on the free bags, later we were able to buy our own by the box.

"It wouldn't matter how much we picked up," says Heather. "There was always more. People don't care. They come into the park, let the dog go and sit on the park bench staring at their phone. They don't watch what their dog is doing, it could be pooing, it could be harassing another dog, or jumping all over someone."

"Some days I'm fine, I pick up the poo, I break up the fight, stop a younger or small dog from being frightened by a bigger bully and some days I want to call the owner out," I say. "It makes me so angry."

"What about the one," says Heather, her thoughts now clearly turning towards funnier memories, "who wanted to take the dogs on the bus because she didn't have a car? Or the woman who insisted on carrying her handbag around, while trying to manage four excited dogs straining on their leads!"

"Who do you think was the best?" I ask, names and faces running through my mind.

"Paul was great with the big dogs," says Heather. "Alice could have a dog eating out of her hand with just a few words and she wasn't too bad with the clients as well."

"What about that tall youngster who never smiled unless she was surrounded by dogs? Put her in the dog park and she was a 'Dog Whisperer'. She also took the best photos and videos for the Facebook page."

"What about Lucy, that girl always had a problem getting a key to open a door, and was forever turning up late…"

"But always with a good excuse; a stray dog, a sick kitten, a bird with a damaged wing." I say. "Was she the one who wore those designer tracksuits bottoms with full hair and makeup? She made me feel so scruffy whenever we met at the park."

Then there were all the applicants who applied without reading the ad properly. Most seemed to think 'I love dogs' was enough to get them hired. Don't get me wrong, I love dogs, and I've loved the ten years I've been working with them, but dog walking isn't taking a small white fluffy around the block on a lead. Dog walking is about taking a bunch of exuberant, screaming two-year-olds, who don't speak English, to the most exciting place they can think of and letting them loose for an hour. It's the equivalent of expecting a child who has been told to get their coat, because they're going to the circus, to sit quietly in the back of the car.

We paid above award rates but still, the wages weren't great, and it's one of those unskilled positions that nevertheless needs a level of competence. It's both physical and stressful when you're trying to manage four excited dogs that have been shut up in the house all day. They tend to pull on the lead, jump around in the back of the car, fighting and barking and generally getting in each other's faces. When you do finally pull up at the park, they're fighting to be first out of the car, yapping and pulling you off your feet, straining on their leads, wanting to be first through the park gate.

As I said, dog walking is rarely a career, usually, it's a stepping-stone to somewhere. Some of our dog walkers found the job they'd always wanted, some finished their studies and moved on, others left the state or went overseas. A few kept in touch but in the main, they were people passing through. We knew dog walking wasn't a career choice; they were earning money for Uni, or it was a second job, a change from working indoors or they needed a job in the pet industry as part of a TAFE animal studies course.

"You know one of the best parts of our business..?" The writing has been forgotten for the moment and now we're in full reminiscing mode. "Watching puppies grow up and knowing we were part of their development, helping to shape their behaviour and often becoming their second family."

All About Dogs

I lean back in my chair and let my mind drift back over the last ten years and see all the dogs, all the different breeds, sizes, ages, colours, and personalities. It's given me an insight into the emotional nature of the bond we have with our dogs. Dogs can only be dogs, it doesn't matter how much you spend on dog trainers, behaviourists, dog therapists and vets. A scent hound is going to follow a wonderful smell and ignore your yelling, unless you have put in the hours on good recall training. A bully breed that is pissed off is going to retaliate when pushed, and all you can hope for is that you read the early signs before it locks its jaws around that annoying, yappy, little white fluffy.

A puppy is distracted by the very air passing by and has the attention span of a fly. No point going to the dog park and expecting the miracles you were able to achieve with a single command and a roast chicken treat. Dogs jump unless taught not to, dogs bark when they are happy, sad, excited, lonely, bored, hungry, frightened and any other reason they feel like barking about. Dogs suffer from many of the same emotional issues we do, including separation anxiety, unable to soothe themselves, car sickness. They develop behavioural issues like chasing bikes, frenzied barking at people in hats, being frightened and running away from people on skateboards, snarling and showing their teeth when strangers approach the car they're locked in.

Dogs, like children, have a specific development timeline and at each stage, predictable behaviour can be controlled and modified with training to meet acceptable conduct and manners. A dog left untrained is a danger to itself and to the people it comes into contact with. All dogs have the ability to become vicious in the right circumstance, just like us. We like to think we are civilised and as domesticated as our family pet, but we can all commit physical violence when backed into a corner, in the protection of those we love, or protecting our possessions, even if that is just a measly old bone.

When I was a child our pets had animal names; dogs were called, Tip, Laddie, Finn, Spot, Whisky, Fido, Teddy, Rex. When we bought the business the dogs we walked had human names; Howard, Jessie, George, Lucy, Freddy, Max, Oscar, Charlie, and were being treated like the 'baby'. Dogs weren't the family pet anymore, they were the 'family'. Rather than expecting the dog to be a 'watchdog', the modern dog was given an emotional support role. For many of our clients, their dog was more than even a companion animal, they were the substitute baby, family, friend. We have seen dogs elevated in their position in the household, not because they have been trained to perform more tasks but because the owner needed more emotional support to handle the stress of their job, financial pressure, social expectations, lifestyle.

I've seen so many people out of touch with who they are, separated from their unique Self, their Inner Self, working in jobs that demand they put their values aside to fall in with the company culture, for the sake of the job, for climbing the promotion ladder. They are workaholics, stressed, with no idea how to self-nurture or self-care. They work, they eat, they sleep, and sometimes the only unconditional emotional comfort and connection they have or allow themselves is the relationship they have with their dog, their 'baby'.

I believe this emotional need has seen the rise and dominance in speciality mix-breeds like the Cavoodle or Labradoodle, Cockapoo, with their 'teddy bear' looks and big round head, large eyes, button nose, soft ears, and floppy puppy-like limbs. They are pretty and cute and melt our heart, especially when they are puppies. Even full-grown, they have a soft floppy body that cries out to be picked up and cuddled. It makes us all gooey inside, a cuteness overload.

There's nothing wrong with getting a dog because you feel lonely or stressed or unable to cope, but sometimes the lack of love, attention, and the emotional unwellness of the owner is passed to the dog. A new puppy needs a lot of attention and while we might remember how easy the family dog of our childhood was, it was probably because mum and dad did all the work. Becoming a parent and getting a puppy is similar; you need to care and protect your puppy, you need to socialise and train it in manners and what is socially acceptable.

Becoming a new dog owner is to become a new parent and you need to think about a parenting course, puppy school, and behavioural training. You need to find a vet, a dog walker, a dog groomer, pet feed store and boarding kennels if you want to go away overnight or on holiday. If your puppy is brought up with confidence, persistence and consistent handling, you'll have the unconditional love and emotional bond you're seeking. If you just go in for cuddles and don't give your pet the training and attention it needs, you end up with a dog that lacks confidence outside the home, which can be passive-aggressive – frightened, so it barks and growls when meeting or seeing other dogs - or it can be uncontrollable when walking on or off the lead.

Dog walkers see the effects on the dog when an owner has done the parenting correctly and we aren't dog trainers, however, we have always offered to work with the trainer or behaviourist the owner has called in. The most upsetting, emotionally unstable dogs are those that are unable to be left alone, that suffer from 'separation anxiety'. When we pass our neediness on to our pet we make them anxious and over time that may mean they need medication to deal with the stress they feel when left behind when the owner goes to the office, drives off to work, or doesn't come home at a regular time. Many of these dogs are on the same anti-anxiety medication as people. Dogs can suffer from anxiety caused by thunderstorms, fireworks, vehicle travel, vet visits, being left with unknown people or put into kennels. The more insecure your puppy is, the less confident your dog will be and the more anxiety it is likely to suffer.

Not only do we have the wonderful job of walking and socialising the new puppy, we often see that dog through to the end of its life. It's heart-wrenching when an owner has to deal with a beloved dog's death. The emotional attachment is so strong that grief can be overwhelming and often it is only other pet owners who understand the loss an owner is feeling. For some it was old age, others a road accident or illness. In the ten years I've been working with dogs and owners I've seen a rise in the cancer rates in client's pets and where in my childhood we could expect a dog to live well into its twenties, now we congratulate an owner for getting their dog past fourteen or fifteen years. Our dogs are suffering from all the same health issues we are; stress, environment, the wrong food, and for some dogs, unethical breeding practices.

However, at the same time as this is the bad news for dogs, the good news is that all aspects of the pet industry are spending more time and money on improving the type of food we feed our dogs, more natural diets of raw meat and soft bone. Improvements in our understanding of dog behaviour, moving away from the old fashioned idea that the dog is the domesticated wolf and a pack animal. We are treating dogs like the social animals they are where the leader is the dog that can keep social cohesion, can maintain relationships and family harmony. Dog trainers are now telling us that domination is not being the leader, it's being a bully, and the position of leadership is one of parental equality.

Some Facts

"Did you know the Australian pet industry is worth about twelve billion dollars?" I'm looking around on Google, researching some facts and figures about the industry for the book.

"I wish we had a bigger slice of the pie, then," says Heather. She's always a bit down, checking the bank balance.

"This article reports the pet industry is one of the fastest growing sectors, with exciting new innovative markets in natural and holistic dog food because of the growing understanding that dogs need breed-appropriate food like raw meat and bone."

"Haven't I been saying that for years?" Heather's checking invoices online. "If only we could reach the dog and cat owners who are killing their pets with kindness and over-feeding them with cheap shit from the supermarket."

I can tell by the way her voice has changed Heather's found something that's going to need a call to the bookkeeper. It's a tone that makes me feel I have to cheer her up, make things right, step in and take control.

"It says here there's an increase in alternative healing practices like Reiki for dogs, and other forms of massage, acupuncture and herbal remedies."

"You'd think people could read invoices; if it says paid, don't pay it again. I'm going to have to ring the bookkeeper to sort this out. I get so sick of having to explain! It's simple; I raise an invoice for your booking, and it's automatically paid because you have your card set up in the system. Then you receive an invoice paid receipt and we're done." She sighs heavily.

"Do you want to hear what else is going on in the pet industry?" I ask, already knowing the answer.

"No. I'm going to ring Annie and get this sorted." She jumps up from her chair, scaring the pups who were sleeping together in their bed under the desk.

I read on. There's been improvements in the manufacture and design of dog harnesses as training aids, to stop dogs pulling on their leads. There's new outdoor adventure gear, mainly by the Americans, protective clothing for the snow and mountain hiking. Innovative wet weather jackets and bootees. This brings to mind the videos of dogs in bootees for the first time and their comic attempts to walk on two legs, booted toes swinging about their heads.

There's a long list in the article, research into dog cancer, spinal surgery for breeds like the Dachshund, the change of attitude and by-laws by apartment strata, allowing people to have pets, subscription boxes with monthly deliveries of pet food, surprise boxes of toys supplied by newly launched unique brands with organic options of treats and samples of feline and canine meals, all aimed at the pet owner who wants to get in on the new wave of retail trends and options available, advertised as making dog and pet ownership more acceptable, easier and more fun.

The Growing Team

There was some resistance from our clients at first, about bringing on staff and building a team. They were used to us walking their dog or caring for their pets and they were hesitant and unsure of having that turned over to what was in their eyes, a stranger. We needed to do some work around reassuring them and showing they would be getting the same professional services, the same high standard of attention and care for their pets as Heather and I delivered.

"What do you think our client's main concern was when we started to take on more dog walkers, Heather?" I'm pulling her away from a tutorial on bread making.

"I don't think anyone likes to change." Her attention is on the woman kneading dough. "The newsletters helped."

I'd forgotten about the newsletters. I'd agonised over the wording of those newsletters for hours. We needed to explain our new plan, the changes we wanted to make, and we needed the clients to come along on the journey. We needed to bring people into the business, not only to help physically but also to give Heather and me the space to concentrate on developing and growing the business.

In Business Together

It was hard to let go and trust someone else to do the job well. We trained the new team members, we walked them through every step of the day from picking up the keys at our house and checking their schedule on their phone, to each home, each dog, each dog park. We showed them the way to secure the dogs in the back of the car, where each dog liked to sit, who was a special buddy with whom. We showed them dog handling videos on YouTube, took them through the staff manuals and when they said they were confident about going out alone, we still micromanaged their first week.

I do want to tell you about our very first employee and team member. She was an amazing young woman who set the bar very high for everyone we interviewed and hired for the next seven years. I'm going to call her Sally. She was intelligent, warm, funny, passionate about animals and training to be a vet nurse. She became the backbone of the team we built, and not only did she help train everyone who came after her, but she also was able to manage the day to day running of the office so Heather and I could take holidays and have the odd weekend away.

Writing this and remembering her, I'm also remembering the incidents that only seemed to happen to Sally. Opening the door to a client's house to pick up a dog and being greeted by the client's father-in-law, naked, walking down the hallway to the guest bedroom. Locking herself in a client's courtyard, something about an inner gate and the keys being left on the kitchen sink. Crawling in through a dog door and out via a bathroom window. I know, it would be irritating and cause for dismissal in some people but with Sally it was funny and part of her innocence and joy for living. She was light relief in a time when we were still coping with the growing pains of the business. Her skills with the dogs and pets were matched by her ability to win over the clients with her knowledge and drive to become a qualified vet nurse.

"Sorry, you were saying...?" The bread-making video is finished, and Heather is ready to turn her attention back to me. "About the people we've employed, the team members."

"I think I've finished," I say, sitting back and enjoying the feeling of having completed another chapter.

"Did you say we couldn't have managed without a great team?" asks Heather, getting up and turning the oven on. "Did you talk about Sally?" On goes the kettle. "Did you talk about how it took us years to learn how to interview and choose the right people?" She turns to me.

"Yes, I think I've covered it."

"Did you talk about how we got to recognise the red flags but not until we'd had to deal with some real crazies, like that ex horse-trainer woman who seemed like the perfect employee but turned into this lesbian-hating, not able to work in a team, can't do it, mad woman. I still don't know what set her off. One day she's driving around in her van walking dogs like she's born for the job and the next she's threatening to sue us."

"Yep, pretty sure I've covered it."

9

Caring For The Cat

"I'm leaving for the airport at four, so if you could feed Fluffy at five, please."

It's not true that cats can't tell the time. They know when it's dinner time, and they'll let you know, wrapping themselves around your ankles, meowing, clawing up your legs and jumping onto the bench under your nose. They don't complain if you're early. Heather and I learnt this and many other cat and small animal facts, including rabbits, guinea pigs, rats, fish, and lizards, providing a pet sitting service over our ten years in business.

Pet sitting is a high-demand, competitive business. People are always looking to escape for the weekend, and while they might take the dog, very few pet owners would want to take the cat, guinea pig or bird. Having someone visit their home and feed their pet is the simplest and most straightforward way to deal with the issue. It was a service once offered by all vet clinics, but few are doing it now, as the cost and staffing can be difficult. Catteries remain an option, but as most are on the outskirts of the city, owners prefer to leave their pet in the comfort and safety of their own home and avoid a long drive.

The service we offer is to visit your home as often as required, to clean the pet bowls or cage, put out fresh water and food, clean or refresh litter trays, bring in newspapers and mail, water indoor or courtyard plants. Over time we have offered this service and we've seen a rise in the popularity of uncaged indoor rabbits, indoor penned guinea pigs, and a variety of sized glass tanks for bearded dragons. Part of our service was not only care for the pet, we're also able to reassure the client everything back home is safe and secure.

Recently we have seen a rise in the number of clients needing pet sitting, not just for the usual overnight, weekend or holiday trip, but also because their job involves regular interstate or overseas business trips. Some clients receive very short notice of an upcoming trip, so we developed a non-booking twenty-four-hour service where a text message was enough to trigger a once or twice daily visit to feed the cat or other pets. We only needed to hold a set of house keys.

"Remember that time we called the police because the client's sliding glass back doors were smashed, and thieves had broken in?"

"Don't tell me... You're writing about pet sitting." Heather hasn't read the story so far, but I do keep interrupting what she is doing to reminisce or ask questions.

"Yes, I remember, but it was Christmas, and they'd targeted the whole street."

Christmas is the busiest pet sitting time, along with the school holidays and Easter. It's one of the things I noticed as a New Zealander; Australia does have more public holidays which is great for our business. We charge double for public holidays whereas we don't add an extra cost to weekend work - something we often have to defend and explain.

"I was thinking about that woman who wanted us to visit her home morning and night over the five days of Christmas but argued that the cost was a complete rip-off." Heather is working at the kitchen bench, preparing something with eggplant for dinner. "I suggested we visit the cats once a day or skip the public holidays by leaving extra food the day before."

"Wasn't the problem she wanted the cats let out in the morning and locked back in at night?"

"Yes, and I suggested they stayed locked in the house to cut costs."

"And she said, we didn't understand how much she needed a holiday and should reduce the price accordingly!"

"And I said I wouldn't be spending Christmas with my grandchildren and the cost barely compensated for that."

It's an issue for some people and not for others. The majority of pet owners are delighted to have a professional feed their cat, rabbit, fish or bird while they are away. It means a relaxing holiday, not having to worry about their pet. For others, they seem to think it's a five-minute job and should almost be a free service. We go to great lengths to explain and give a comprehensive service. We see ourselves as a substitute parent for a much-loved family

In Business Together

member while the family is away. We put the needs of the pet, as a business, above our own. We offer a service where we are entrusted with the house keys to visit the home once or twice a day. We follow the feeding and care instructions, possibly give mediation or prepare a special diet.

However, you might feel hiring the schoolgirl neighbour is cheaper and having her pop in daily is sufficient. And fingers crossed nothing goes wrong. But if your pet becomes ill, you want an experienced professional who will recognise that and act quickly, getting the animal to your vet. You need someone who can react professionally in an emergency. To notice if a door has been tampered with, a window broken, a toilet overflowing. Maybe the electricity is off and not heating your tank of tropical fish, or defrosting the fridge-freezer.

I'm staring at Heather working at the kitchen bench without really seeing her. I know that she's wearing her favourite apron; it has the back view of a large naked lady cooking. I'm thinking about pet sitting and how it's just part of our day now, part of the schedule. It's like Heather preparing the vegetables - she doesn't have to think about how to peel the carrots or which knife to use to cut up the cauliflower, so it fits into the middle-sized pot. Heather has been preparing vegetables long enough to do it without thinking. Pet sitting has become like that. But it wasn't always.

Always Put The Keys In Your Pocket

Rule one is to carry the house keys on your person *at all times*, don't put them down, not on the client's hall table, kitchen bench, or washing machine. The cost of a locksmith can instantly cancel a weekend's income. I didn't do it often, but often enough in those early years to make me sick to my stomach when I realised I'd closed the front door and didn't have the house keys in my pocket. It is the worst feeling. The pet locked inside, the client overseas, and you've just closed the door to the house.

When I started, there was so much to remember I wrote a checklist.
- Always keep the keys in your pocket
- If you turn on a light, turn it off when leaving
- Wash all pet bowls and tidy the feeding area
- Wash the spoon or other utensils used and return to the drawer or leave on the bench
- Clean litter tray or refresh tray, put litter bag back where it belongs
- Gather all rubbish, from the litter tray, cans or food pouches, dry food boxes and remove from the property
- Clean kitchen sink and bench
- Sweep food and litter tray areas
- Take a photo of the pet
- Bring in newspaper and mail, water plants if requested
- Send photo and message to the client
- Check everything is as you found it
- Have house keys in your hand when you exit the house and the property

I don't have the checklist now; it's ingrained, fixed, routine, the norm, just like noticing anything that's changed since I was in the house the day before. A sweep of the room will alert me to cat vomit under the table, chair, on the rug. Has a bored feline emptied the rubbish bin? A door closed that might have trapped the rabbit. A hole in the water container. A suspicious noise.

We ask clients if anyone else is going to be in the house while we are pet sitting. It's always weird to work around someone staying in the home while the owner is on holiday. I've worked around friends, relations, a partner or grown child. Scooped out the litter tray and opened a tin of cat food while an adult lay on the couch watching television. The question in my mind is always - why aren't they saving the cost of the pet sitting by having their guest care for the cat, rabbits, mice, fish?

In the same way, I find it peculiar to be employed to feed a pet at five o'clock when the owner left for the airport at four o'clock.

All About The Cats

In my experience cats fall into one of three groups, the smoochy ones who want attention, cuddles and are happy to be patted and brushed, who rub around your ankles as you open the tin to feed them. The aggressive ones that hiss the moment you walk into their territory and you not only can't approach them, but you also need to protect yourself. These fearsome creatures will fly at you, corner you in a room, come at you with claws and teeth. I arm myself with a spray bottle of water and a pillow when I feed these angry cats. Lastly, there are the ones you never see. These cats are so shy they hide as soon as they hear the key in the door. Some might, over time, show the tip of their tail or the top of their ears. I have had a situation where, over two years, I never saw the cat but knew they were there, because the food was eaten. The litter tray was used. I don't try to find a hiding cat; I give them their privacy.

Cats are about as different from each other as their owners. There are the messy ones who spread litter not only around the litter tray and the room it's in, but tramp it through the house. Some cats can't eat a meal without dragging it out of the food bowl but also off the pretty plastic food mat and onto the floor. Ants love these kinds of cats and when I return, it's to a moving black mass that needs a great deal of cleaning up. Some of this messy eating is because of the type of food we feed cats now. When I was a child, we fed our family cat roughly chopped gravy beef. It was a cheap cut of meat, and while my mother cooked it with onion, carrots and dumplings for the family, Mittens had hers raw. Today, we feed conveniently tinned and pouched pet food which is mainly soy-based with a very liquid gravy. And while Mittens lived to the then average of between twenty-two and twenty-five, today's cats have a life expectancy of eighteen to twenty.

"Do you think I should do a rant about the food people feed cats?" It's late in the day, and my shoulders and neck are aching. I need to stop writing, but I keep telling myself, just one more paragraph.

"We do feel strongly about the link between obesity, diabetes, cancer, and young cats having their teeth removed, and the processed wet food and the dry kibble and biscuits they're fed." Heather says.

"People are changing. More web sites are selling natural pet food, more videos on how to prepare pet food using raw meat, organ meat, soft raw bone, fish." I'm doing stretches as I talk, arms above my head. "There are good all-natural brands from New Zealand, and we've seen more of our owners are buying that rather than supermarket specials."

It's a continuing discussion we've had since we started. Heather had changed her dog Alex and cat Henry's diet when she found a book on raw meat and raw soft bone. The famous story about Henry is that he held out twelve days from eating the new food in his bowl. We don't know how old he would have lived to be on his new diet, as in the early hours of the morning he slipped off the neighbour's roof and broke his back. We sadly made the only decision possible and put him down.

"Have you written about those houses where everything is cat themed; the pictures on the walls, the fridge magnets, the tea towels, pot plant holders with pink cat ears, china cat figurines." She shakes her head.

"Well, that's better than the places where I stand outside to take my last clean air breath and have to brace myself to go inside."

Cats can be messy, and so can people. The majority of homes I go into are tidy, but the odd one isn't. I know that hoarding is an emotional disease, and there are levels to which the condition can affect people, but I find these homes the most challenging. The smell, the bags of rubbish, the spider webs, the mouse dirt, the narrow lane between 'stuff' to reach the pet bowls and litter tray is distressing. I find the living circumstances for the client very upsetting, but worse is the filth the cat is living in, bowls coated in a crust of old dried food, slime-filled water bowls, litter trays awash with urine and faeces. These homes are shocking, challenging to enter, and while I feel the need to shower when I get home, my heart goes out to the poor souls who live in those unhappy circumstances.

While the above example is difficult to understand, even harder to comprehend are the homes that show the owner has spared no expense on personal comforts. At the same time, they feed the cat the cheapest, poorest quality, processed food. The litter tray is not adequate for the cat's needs and the stench of ammonia when I walk in the front door shows the owner hasn't bothered to keep it clean.

Cleaning, My Obsession

"Stop cleaning, walk away now." I'm entirely on my hands and knees, trying to get the area around the food bowls clean.

"Maybe I could leave a damp cloth over it and have another go in the morning." We're looking after an old cat who is messy with her food, in part because she only has a couple of teeth left.

"Leave it. If there was a vacuum cleaner at hand I swear you'd clean their entire house," says Heather, irritation creeping into her voice. "We are employed to care for the pet, just leave the housework to the owner."

I hate leaving cats to eat out of dirty food bowls. I like the food mat and surrounding area to be clean. I'm just as particular about the litter tray and surroundings. Most litter trays are open plastic boxes, sometimes with a plastic lining, and kept in the bathroom or laundry, although the modern apartment laundry is little more than a cupboard built around the washing machine and dryer. There are hooded litter trays which are advertised as keeping the litter contained and eliminating smell. Unless the hooded trays are cleaned every day and refreshed with new litter every five to seven days, the cat is forced to the toilet in an ammonia-filled chamber. There have been times when just taking the lid off a hooded tray has made my eyes water. I believe cats and all pets want to be clean and healthy, so it's up to us to care for them properly.

An Unusual Request

It was an extraordinary request for a client to make and only ever happened that once. First, there was a two-week booking to visit Felix once a day. Not an unusual request; we had been caring for the overweight, spoiled black cat with white bib, belly and toes for over five years. The owners were a lovely couple, she was American, and he was Australian. The bookings always came through in her name and were typically made a couple of weeks in advance. This new request was no different until the email.

She, Felix's other parent, had an unusual request but we were under no obligation to say yes. They were flying to Bali to meet extended family for a grand holiday. Having been together over ten years and not wanting a big fuss, they had decided on a registry office wedding and would surprise everyone with the announcement on their arrival. The only problem was they needed two witnesses. So, they asked us, their pet sitters.

Heather and I were a bit taken aback and then very excited. It seemed we only had to turn up at the registry office on Saturday morning at nine o'clock, sign the official papers and take photos on their phones for them.

"Do you remember what we wore?" I ask Heather.

"What, to the wedding?" Heather muses. "I don't know. You would have gone through the wardrobe and decided if we needed something new."

She's probably right, and I can't remember either, but it would have been a combination of trousers and a shirt. I know we talked about taking a bottle of bubbles, a card, flowers, a gift. We ordered a handcrafted pottery bowl with Felix's name around one side and the date of the wedding around the other. The bowl was to be black and white with a picture of Felix as well.

The bride and groom were late and ran up the stairs to where we were waiting. We were so glad to see them. We'd begun to think we were in the wrong place! Hugs, kisses, apologies over, we were ushered into a small office with a wooden desk pushed into one corner, a crammed bookcase in the other and the front windows open to the noise of traffic. It was a scaled-back ceremony, no music, a vase of flowers and the bunch we gave to the bride, the official in a dark suit and his secretary hovering at his side, passing papers and a pen. Vows and rings were exchanged, more hugs and kisses, photographs and it was all over. The newlywed couple left in a taxi for the airport in a flurry of excitement, and Heather and I, feeling a little deflated, drove home to change into our uniforms and begin work.

We would take good care of Felix in their absence.

10

Our Glue

"I don't know how to cover the middle years."

"What do you mean the 'middle years'?" Heather is driving, we're caught in traffic and not moving.

"Those years when we finally had it together and the business was ticking over, we had a team, things between us were okay, we'd renovated the house, you'd stopped freaking out about going broke and losing the house. You know, when things got normal."

"You mean when you finally gave up all those crazy ideas you had, selling shampoo, that 'Smelly Dog' cologne, handcrafted leather collars, the imported herbal remedies, the expensive one-off pottery pet bowls with personalised pet names and the books you wrote." She looks over at me. "What a waste of money all that was."

In Business Together

"We sold stuff, I was trying to diversify, bring on another income stream, all the business blogs on Google said that would spread the income load. And we could have sold heaps more shampoo and those great wide-toothed combs if you'd offered them to your grooming clients." This is an old argument.

"Don't start, I told you. I'm not a salesperson. I don't like selling. I'm shy, not pushy."

"That's a laugh - when we go to the park you're always wandering off, talking to someone, getting in their ear about how their dog is overweight and should be on a raw meat diet, or giving training tips or showing them how they've got the wrong harness on." I know Heather is passionate about a dog's diet and the food owners feed their dogs. She can't help herself. When she sees an overweight dog waddling around the park she has to have a quick word with the owner.

"Dog boarding was the worst idea." Heather rolls her eyes. "Thank goodness we don't do that anymore."

"But you liked the money, didn't you?"

It started with helping a client with a bulldog. She'd been asked to a family event and couldn't find a kennel to take Harry. We'd immediately said we couldn't, the dog was too big, the house too small; with a hankie-sized backyard, we simply couldn't. And then called her back and said yes. We had no idea what we started, but the news spread faster than fire through the dry bush. Dog owners didn't want to put their dogs in kennels way out in the country, they wanted them in the city and somewhere they could sleep on the couch and be part of the family.

Well, one thing led to another, one dog became four and then seven. We provided the food, the client dropped off and picked up their pet and we charged in the same way as a hotel, from check-in until check out at noon the following day at a fixed rate. Over the next four years, we never had a day when there wasn't at least one and more often, three extra dogs staying in the house. At the time we still had Alex, Heather's little brown staffy.

Christmas was the busiest time for dog boarding, and we had our regular clients who booked from one year to the next. The number crept up, one year we had six, then eight, and when we had twelve over a ten-day period, Heather finally said no more! We did have rules around who we accepted for boarding. All dogs had to be spayed or fixed, no dogs taller than Heather's knees; we'd once had a massive Great Dane who rested her head on the dining table when we ate! Dogs had to be toilet trained, well, tell that to the couch, they were perfect at home and the moment they came to stay they pissed and shit wherever they liked. No special diets, everyone ate the same food, but we did give medication when required.

"What about those videos," I remember. "Christmas morning, me in the spare room, surrounded by dogs on the bed. There was hardly room for me to turn over."

"And then you came up with the puppy idea."

"I felt guilty not walking dogs and being home all day."

"You were running the office, managing all the admin, social media, the newsletter, bookings and all that other stuff, you didn't need to anymore."

In Business Together

I felt bad about sitting at the computer all day, so I let it be known I'd look after puppies who hadn't had their final vaccines and couldn't yet go to doggy day-care. Leaving little puppies under three or four months is a big problem for most new puppy owners. The pup is used to mum and siblings and so they cry and get into mischief. I didn't think they'd be much trouble, as we have a concrete floor; most pups aren't good at toileting until they're closer to twelve months, and I could make sure they had a couple of small meals during the day. Puppies need small regular meals until they are close to a year old.

"Plus all those puppies," I say, "were moved across into our dog walking, so it was a no brainer."

The traffic begins to move. Sitting together in the car seems to be our only time for intimacy, driving between jobs, picking up dogs, feeding cats, meeting new clients. There's so much else to do at home, the business, the housework, taking care of our own pets. I watch a constant stream of houses pass out the window. They are all the same, a bit less garden, a brick front wall instead of a hedge.

"We don't fight as much." I'm not sure where this thought comes from or why I say it. "I seem to remember a lot of banging of cupboard doors, tense silence and loud crashing." I know in the early days I was a little intimidated by the anger and the noise of Heather letting off steam, working out her frustration. They trigger flashbacks of my childhood and the violent relationships I used to get myself into.

"I didn't know any other way, and I'd never had a partner point out my behaviour." Heather is staring straight ahead. "I thought it was normal, well, it was normal for me."

"I think by the time we met and began to live together we were older and wiser," I say. "More willing and able to look at our own and each other's behaviour and how it impacted each other. Besides, I'd had years of examining my behaviour, with counsellors, in my journals, it was part of my sobriety."

"It was all new to me." Heather's creeping the van forward, waving a red car in ahead of us. "I wasn't used to talking about how I felt or how I was acting. You pointing out I was slamming doors and asking what was going on caught my off guard. Most of the time I wasn't even aware I was slamming cupboard doors." There's a grin on her face.

Talking about how we felt wasn't an overnight fix, I think we argued and lost patience with each other for the first few years. Not only were we not used to living with someone, but we also didn't know how to resolve issues, in our personal lives or in the business. Sometimes I don't think we even knew if we were arguing about a personal issue or a business problem, as they just merged into a knot of irritation that we didn't have the willingness or ability to work through. Most of the time we were tired. Not the type of tiredness that needs an early night, but the deep weariness that needs a three month holiday, which we were in no position to take.

"And then we seemed to just stop." I'm aware of crossing my arms. "One day everything was difficult, and we didn't seem to be able to come to a reasonable compromise on anything and then we were just working things out and making joint decisions."

"You wore me down with your constant need to talk about every little thought or action, everything was analysed, dissected, every thought or emotion followed back to some childhood drama, some family behaviour, attributed to some a past relationship or partner." Heather's driving through the lights and we're finally out of the traffic snarl. "I've never met anyone who pulls everything apart, looking for reasons and wanting explanations of *why*. I've just been me and never thought about it."

"Were you happy with feeling all that pent-up anger, feeling frustrated and not understanding why you were acting the way you were?"

"No, but that's not the point," says Heather.

"I didn't want you to change but you were always just exploding, and you didn't seem to understand why." I say, remembering how reactionary I had been in those early years, knowing in my head Heather wasn't going to lash out at me but still feeling uncomfortable with the level of her anger.

"Don't you act like you don't have a temper." She raises her eyebrows at me.

I have to laugh, Heather's grinning and I'm squirming, knowing I can shout and slam doors with the best of them. But I was always aware I had greater knowledge about my reactions and behaviour than Heather did, and I was in a better position to take control and tease out what the real issue was. I'd had more practice at self-evaluation, and I had more patience than Heather will ever have.

"I think," I say, "that we each bring different strengths to the relationship and the partnership. Sometimes I'm not so aware of them but that's what everyone says. Maybe because they're on the outside they see them more clearly. I know you are more concerned about rules and doing the right thing. I know the majority of the time you're more black and white than I am. You're less likely to think outside the box."

"I've changed," says Heather. "I'm more comfortable with myself. I was shy and I decided to pretend I wasn't, and I think I became this other person and now I think I've come back to being myself, a little shy in some circumstance but mostly happy about who I am."

"That's the best part of our relationship," I agree, jumping on this insight from Heather. "We have come through the early years and have become ourselves, have allowed each other to be who we really are or who we feel ourselves to be and to be comfortable with that person."

"I'm still not good at saying how I feel," Heather admits. "Most of the time if you ask, my mind shuts down, goes blank and I have no idea what to say."

"So, where does that leave us? I have to write something in the book."

"I love you."

"Okay, but what does that really mean, you love your bed, you love cooking, you love your dog and you spoil him." Heather is smitten with Taco, the black and tan Chihuahua we took in when a client needed to rehome him and his house sister, Beans.

"Respect," she says firmly. "We respect each other." There's a change in her voice. "I think that's why we're still together, still in love because we have respect for each other."

"It's a willingness for me," I say. "A willingness to be open, to listening, to thinking about change. A willingness to be present, a willingness to change. I think that's something I learnt when I was doing 12-Step."

"We never knowingly wanted to hurt each other." Heather's on a roll now.

"I never want to hurt you. Is that love?"

"Understanding, caring, being equal, listening to what is going on for each other." Heather smiles. "That's our glue, what's kept us together."

"Well, aren't you the romantic when you get started?" We grin at each other.

It's always like this between us. The most important conversations, the most intimate, take place in the car. Whether it's sorting out problems with a client, a team member, making a business decision or having a 'heart to heart', it happens when we're going somewhere. It's as if we find safety together in the car, a vehicle bubble without the distractions we have at home. Or maybe it's true what they say about being more creative if the main area of the brain is busy doing something, like driving in Sydney traffic.

"Money," I say. "That's always been a fundamental difference between us. It's your security, gives you safety, is measurable. I've never had money and I value different things when it comes to security and safety."

"Home, that's where you feel safe, that's where you run."

"And yet," I say, "every home I've ever had has been provided by someone else. Rentals, in relationships, living in your house is the perfect example."

"*Our* house," says Heather.

Money, what gives us a feeling of security and safety, has been a fundamental difference right from the start and the basis of many arguments. We have different ideas and different values about money. I initially thought Heather was a miser and made jokes about her unwillingness to open her purse. Heather believed I had no regard for money and spent it willy-nilly without thought. I think over the years we've reached an understanding of how each of us feels about money, its use, its value, its importance. We don't argue about it now.

The difference about where our security and safety comes from does still cause disagreements. I don't believe in having the amount of insurance cover that Heather has. I think it's giving money to big business and it's closer to gambling than a surety. I'd rather bank the money. She feels safer having life insurance, income protection, full health cover. It's as much a class difference as a difference in the value we put on money. I've never had enough money for anything more than basic car insurance.

While we had differing views on money, neither of us had a head for figures and in the ten years of being in business together have always been totally reliant on our bookkeeper and accountant. We've never had a workable budget or had financial forecasts or known the full cost of any of our services or outgoings. Where every business coach talks about the importance of knowing your numbers, neither Heather nor I have fully understood that side of our business.

"I know when we were first talking about buying the business, I rattled off the things we had in common that would make us great business partners, like work ethic. We're both babies of the fifties and don't need someone telling us to get up and go to work. We're self-motivated, able to work without direction, we've both been in leadership roles. Although that does sometimes cause problems." It's my turn to grin. My leadership style can sometimes look like bossiness or bullying.

"I've had those roles," says Heather. "But really I'm a follower by heart. Happy to let someone else give direction. I agonise over decisions. My preferred action is to procrastinate."

"But how much is that an issue of lack of self-worth?" We've had these conversations over the years, talking about how we feel about ourselves, how past relationships damaged our self-esteem, how family issues affected the view we hold about ourselves and the messages we repeat in our heads. The beliefs we hold about our place in the world and our worthiness to be loved.

Heather's not overly comfortable with these discussions. They have no place in her practical, see, hear, touch, world. It's my interest in all things psychological and how we react and behave that sparks these convoluted conversations that I'm really having on my own. Maybe it's the writer that loves to observe other people's behaviour or my fascination with my reactions to people and events. My Inner Life, Inner World holds more interest than the Outer World and understanding how people tick is part of that obsession.

"Remember that first counsellor we went to?" I break into the silence. "I'm not sure she was helpful, I thought she might give us a clearer picture of how to have an intimate relationship while trying to get our heads around being new business owners."

"I think she was good," says Heather. "She got us talking, communicating."

I can't help but smile at her admission. Getting Heather to even agree to talk to a counsellor had been a major coup. It seemed her father didn't think much of counsellors and he'd passed his views on to his daughter.

"Now you do, but you didn't at the time."

"Well, in all fairness it was all new to me," says Heather. "It was okay for you, you'd been going to counsellors for years, you felt comfortable talking to them, you didn't think of them as strangers or as divulging personal business."

"The problem is when there's something blocking us from being able to move forward in the business or make changes in our personal life, you want to knuckle down and not budge. Procrastination and stubbornness!"

Heather lifts an eyebrow. "And you're bossy and always right."

"Good to know," I say in a silly voice. "Do you think this is what I should write in the book?"

"Yes, you can say we made a lot of mistakes at the start, but we didn't lose the house, we didn't lose the business, and ten years later we still love each other. Isn't that what your book's about?"

11

We Sell Up

"Let's get back to talking about your relationship, not the business."

It's a Thursday evening and we're at our first appointment with the counsellor. I'm sitting at one end of the sofa, close to tears, and Heather is at the other. While we are both in an open body posture, slightly turned to each other, arms dangling, hands in laps, I'm not sure we aren't feeling shut down to each other.

The opening pleasantries are over, and the first question has been asked; why are we here? Heather is quiet and I launch into the silence with an emotional appeal for an understanding of my fears and apprehension of our soon to be new circumstance, living without the business in a different state.

"What are the tears, Hannah?"

I look away, trying to put words to the enormous ball of aggravation and alarm rolling around in my belly. It's been there for so long I'd forgotten how and when it started. It's not the first time I've felt it, it seems familiar and yet I don't know what it is.

"I'm scared that when we sell the business we won't have a relationship."

These are the only words I can find to begin to unravel my mixed emotions. It's not everything I feel, there's resentment, but that also feels old. There's some self-hate, as if I've sold myself down the river once again.

"I want to write," I blurt out.

I've wanted to write ever since that first story my mother patiently typed up on her gossamer writing paper, correcting my spelling, a full twelve chapters. She'd also drawn a picture on the front cardboard cover for me to colour in. I was so proud of myself. My story was based on the work of Enid Blyton, four children; two boys, two girls, and a dog. Dad read my work and remarked that the children spent a lot of time eating. I was offended and years later, still smarting over his response, wished I'd been able to say, "Well, I could hardly talk about your father sexually abusing me."

"No one's talking about stopping you from writing," says Heather. "We're selling the business and finally going to start a new life, just you and I, and our dogs."

"I know, I know, it's me. I feel as if we won't know each other once the business goes and we haven't had the relationship we promised we were going to have."

Even the counsellor looks perplexed by my response. She knows we've been living together for ten years and were married two years ago. She looks like she's going to ask a question but then just lets the silence fill the room. She's not a talker. Not in the way some counsellors are, always interrupting, probing, giving their interpretation, vital feedback and reflections. She sits, waiting, giving us the space to find our own words.

"I want…" But what do I want? I'm the one who went looking for a counsellor, who booked the appointment, who made a fuss about needing to talk to someone and now I can't find the words, I'm so choked up with this thing. This thing in my belly.

I'm not sure what this new relationship will look like and I need to know. Relationships have always been so dicey with their hidden agendas, with the other person's needs always coming first. That's on me, I do that, meeting other people's needs has always been part of my emotional makeup. It's hard to see because I'm always so outspoken, so dogmatic about my views, what I think, what I'll do or not do. But that all changes when I'm emotionally tangled, as then the emotional needs of the other become my needs, what they want for their life becomes my goal. I have to write now, I don't have time to pursue Heather's new goal, this new eco-lifestyle with gardening and bottling and bread-making.

My fear is *saying what I want*. How much easier it has been to go along with what I perceive the other person needs. My strength in a relationship has been the ability to meet another's needs. My grandfather had his sexual gratification using my child-body. My father had a son when I became a tomboy. My first lesbian relationship needed a compliant whipping boy and I stayed until the day I realised I wasn't afraid she would kill me but that I might kill her. There have been others, a dozen different scenarios, sometimes our needs were mutual, sometimes not.

From the beginning, Heather and I talked about relationships. We told each other about the relationships we had been in, the good bits and the bad, the pain and hurt, the disappointment when the romantic dream was over. We had not given up on the idea that the perfect relationship was out there. When we fell in love we believed we had found what we had been looking for.

"The last ten years have been amazing. I love you so much and we've done so much together. The business, gaining in confidence and self-esteem. Learning how strong and capable we are. We've proven to ourselves and others we could run the business." I pause, gathering myself to make my point. "But when we started working in the business, I think we put the relationship on hold. I still want that romantic intimacy we said we wanted."

"Again," Heather's face is flushed, "you do this to me. You have the words, you can talk about your feelings, you can talk and talk, and I'm left feeling stupid because when I think about how I feel, I go blank and how I was feeling disappears. I love you, I want us to be happy, I want us to live a new way, without having to go to work, to be tied down seven days a week."

"You said you didn't want me to spend all day on the computer like I do now."

"Yes, because once you get on that computer you never stop. I have to call you three times to come and have dinner, you don't want to go for a walk, come and have coffee, it's always the computer."

"Because you won't talk to me." I'm between tears and anger. This is another well-rehearsed accusation.

Heather chats, she approaches people when we walk our dogs in the park. I can understand she would have been a great bus driver, always chirpy, having a laugh. She likes reading the news online where she used to read the newspaper cover to cover. She remembers all the bus drivers she's worked with and we're often accosted in the supermarket and stop for a catch-up chat. She's like me in respect of friendships, just a few and they're all over twenty years old. She's friendly but not particularly social now, age has caught up with her, but back in the 'good old days', she was part of the pub-going party-crowd.

When Heather meets with friends it's all 'what have you been doing', 'where did you go on holiday', 'what are your plans'. When I spend time with my friends it's 'how are you feeling', 'what are you thinking', 'what are you reading', 'what movies have you seen'. When Heather talks to her friends its social chit-chat with a cold beer. When I talk with friend's it's over coffee and soul revealing. The Outer world vs the Inner world.

"I can't, I can't talk about how I feel all the time. I don't care about all those deep and meaningful thoughts like you do. I don't care why I said this, do that, behave in this way. I don't want to scrutinise everything about me and my personality as you do." Heather's frustration overflows.

"Well, I want more than 'I'm fine', 'I'm okay', 'yeah, great'." Now it's me going red in the face, showing my annoyance at these usual pointless replies to a perfectly sensible question. "I want to know what you are thinking and feeling about what I'm asking."

"There isn't anything going on under what I'm doing. You say shall we do the dishes and I say okay. You say, 'How do you feel about that?' and I say 'Okay'." She throws up her hands.

I have to laugh, it sounds so silly when Heather says this. She's so of the world we live in, so normal, up-front, average, practical, straight up, uncomplicated. I burrow around underground, dissecting, evaluating, constantly looking for some significant unspoken cause and effect.

"I don't think this is getting us anywhere." The counsellor steps in. "Hannah, what are your concerns about selling the business?"

I bring myself back to the problem at hand. "I'm worried that the business has provided us with a structure for our relationship and without the business, there'll be no relationship." I'm sure I said this before. "The business gave us both a way to avoid issues in our relationship, a place to hide. And it also provided the impetus for growth; we had to confront aspects of ourselves when dealing with clients, trying to solve problems, and stay current with business practises."

"So, what are you saying; we won't have a relationship after the business is gone?" Heather's crossing her arms, pushing back against the corner of her end of the sofa.

"No, I'm asking what you think it will look like and how close is that to how I think it will look."

"It'll be the same as it is now."

"I don't think it will, if you think I'm not going to spend time writing and you're talking about gardening and being self-sufficient."

"What are you really frightened of, Hannah, because this isn't making sense."

"If we don't have the business will I be of any use?" I hear myself saying this, the words hang, trembling, in the air. I understand for the first time that I want to be loved for who I am, not what I can do, yet I'm hanging on to the belief that if I don't provide some emotional use I'm not loveable.

"You don't believe I love you," says Heather, moving closer to me on the sofa, reaching out to take my hand. "It's like an unfounded but visceral fear that you are going to be alone, that I don't love you for you, that if you're not helping run the business I have no use for you, that I'm going to throw you out on the street with your suitcase. What else can I do to prove I love you and I want us to move into this new phase of our lives together?"

"What is it you want, Hannah? Tell Heather."

"I want all the usual things. To be loved, to be wanted, to be hugged and kissed. I want a life with you." I'm looking in Heather's eyes, squeezing her hand. "Where we finally have time to play, to have fun, to sleep in, to sit on the back porch and watch your vegetables grow and the dogs chase each other around the fruit trees. I want to be surrounded by friends who understand me, who will celebrate my birthday and come to dinner. I want my grandchildren to visit. I want to write."

"We will have all these things, you can stop treating me like one of your violent ex-partners, in one of those battering relationships, where you're just a punching bag. It hurts when you act like I don't love you."

"I didn't know I was."

"This isn't the end, this is the beginning. You silly woman, come here, I love you."

The Order Of Business

"The sales contract for the business," I say, "will take about three weeks."

Heather and I have been working with the new owner in between dog walking and pet sitting. We've been introducing the new owner to our bookkeeper, passing on the details of our IT guy, the printer we've used for the last ten years, the photographer, the local garage with the best mechanics. There's a pile of paperwork, manuals, client's files, and a box of clients' house keys.

As we pass over the business to the new owner, the file cabinet drawers are emptied, our desks are cleared, one whole side of the guest bedroom is cleared, along with the middle set of drawers. I feel as if a large hole has been made in the middle of the house and we have space to walk around, to dance. It feels light and a relief to finally hand over all the papers, folders, files and documents associated with ten years of business.

The first informative newsletter has been sent to clients, although they have known for over six months the business was on the market. We've suggested a Meet & Greet with nibbles and champagne, for those clients who want to be formally introduced.

We Sell Up

Heather's doing research into properties in Victoria. We're looking for a block bigger than a suburban house and less than a farm property. Established fruit trees and gardens would be nice, a shed and garage a necessity. We need two beds, two baths, a study, internet access, not on the main road. It will need to be fully fenced to keep the cat and dogs safe, plus we might end up with farm animals, Heather's mentioned a cow and a pig. These animals are not to be named or thought of as pets, however, they will be going in the freezer.

"I want to have my own outdoor space," announces Heather, in the middle of cleaning out a box of tax files. "I need a stove, a large wooden bench, shelving for storage and equipment for bottling fruit, pickling vegetables and jam making. I want to bake bread and try anything else I come across on the internet."

I'm shocked by this outburst and request. I knew Heather wanted a garden shed, but a whole outside kitchen workspace, that's new, that's never been talked about. It's another move away from the dependency of working in the business together. I'm both pleased and a little horrified at her stand for independence. Somehow it sounds different to me than when I was saying I wanted a studio, a writing room, a place to go and have some alone time, read a book. The pull me/push me of working together for ten years and now wanting to establish individual interests and hobbies, while revitalising our intimacy, continues to both delight and frighten me.

"Great," I say brightly, hoping the edge of doubt in my voice isn't noticed.

We have until the end of the tax year to complete the hand-over to the new business owner. The house is being painted inside and out, ready to go on the market. Today the painters are outside so Heather and I can go through the last of the boxes we've taken out of the attic. After the painting is completed we'll start clearing our wardrobes and cupboards before we start the packing. It's hard to know if it will all go smoothly, like clockwork, or just be an overwhelmingly stressful experience. We have decided to drive the car to Victoria with the cat and our four Chihuahuas. It's only about eight or nine hours according to Heather, but it might seem longer with George crying in his cat carrier and the pups arguing in the pillowed backseat hammock.

There's so much to do, another meeting with the real estate agent, For Sale signs to go up in front of the house, hand over the business car and final documentation to the new owner, dress the house for the sales video, scan the internet for a prospective new home. I'm eating too much and simultaneously writing a book.

Afterword

"You don't know what you don't know."

These words became our mantra over the ten years Heather and I were in business together. Each time we paid a professional more money than we could afford and didn't receive the promised results, every time we didn't know the correct question to ask to find the right answer, every time we were let down or had the rug pulled out from under us, we would repeat these words.

We accepted this when we went into business with no previous experience or knowledge. We knew we were naive and open to the exploitation of others, and we knew we would make mistakes, sometimes more than once, but we also knew we would learn from them. We gained experience, grew smarter, and gradually started to believe in ourselves and our abilities rather than presuming everyone was more intelligent than we were.

I have one regret. I wish we'd opened a personal savings account on day one and not touched it. Yes, we did put money into our super accounts, and we did renovate our home, took overseas holidays, bought new cars, invested in beautiful pieces of art, had a wonderful commitment ceremony and an equally beautiful wedding. We enjoyed our life together, went to the theatre, the movies, took harbour trips, and dined out. But I still wish we'd opened that savings account.

Another mistake I believe we made was not making decisions and acting quickly enough. Between my snap decisions and Heather's agonising, we often didn't take the opportunities that came up. We look back now and see how we could have saved ourselves time and money, had we agreed and acted sooner. We wish, for instance, we'd sold up and moved interstate years ago.

Our wins, our successes and our accomplishments outweigh any regrets, however. It's been a fantastic ride, a heady combination of growing as a person, as a couple, plus watching and supporting other people to grow and accomplish their dreams. In our ten years of business, we met some amazing people who became friends and acquaintances who added to and enriched our lives.

I'm especially proud that Heather and I were able to help and support those team members who reached their personal and professional goals. I believe we have been mentors and stepping-stones to several young men and women who have a passion for working with animals and are now employed in the pet industry. We always took high school students on Work Experience Week and allowed them to experience first-hand the proper handling of dogs. We gave TAFE students the number of hours required to complete their animal studies certificates and diplomas. We educated pet owners as best we could in the ideal care of their animals.

Afterword

Heather and I have been loyal supporters of local businesses, IT, printers, our excellent photographer, 'the boys' at the garage, the neighbour, who in return for caring for his elderly cat, did all our graphic design. We are current members of the local council small business chapter and have enjoyed many a 'bitch' session over the quarterly-lunches with other home-based businesswomen.

A new relationship, a new business, it seemed we had placed ourselves in a pressure cooker world and now ten years on, Heather and I are changed women. We are more robust, more self-confident, happier, more resilient, more honest and realistic about our strengths and weaknesses. We have come through situations we thought would break us, only to find that together we able capable of handling anything. We've been open and willing to learn, to take chances and have made our dreams a reality.

Ten years ago, I was still dealing with the remnants of my alcoholic, drug addicted life. I was working to put the old life behind me and find a new path, sober. I was looking for a fresh start without fully realising it. If you ask Heather, she will tell you she too was at a crossroads, out of work because of an accident that left her blind in one eye, lost and alone with no clear path forward. What would life have been like for both of us if we hadn't met online and fallen in love? Hand in hand, our leap of faith has been a fantastic love story.

Soul Scribbling

"When the pupil is ready, the teacher will show up."

This has been my experience in my life. I ask the universe for what I want, and She sends me what I need. If I'm open to the change, it's easy and fun. If I'm not, it's difficult and sometimes painful.

This book is about ten years of my life, one decade out of nearly seventy. I had no plans to write it, but the title appeared in my head and refused to leave. I began scribbling down ideas, thoughts, adding larger pieces about my childhood, becoming a parent and grandparent, my years of alcohol and drug addiction. I thought I might be writing a 'Business How-To' or maybe a memoir. I wondered about adding an insight or reflection or spiritual piece after each chapter talking about what I'd learnt.

But the book had a mind of its own, and by the third rewrite, the story was in control, and I wasn't able to direct it, I was merely typing the words as they flowed into my mind.

The story is true, honest and heartfelt. I was happy to write it because I've experienced the difficulty of talking about the reality of working with your intimate other. How your relationship impacts your business and how being in business together can compromise your relationship. I wanted to tell the story of one couples' experience of marriage and business.

While an overview might convince you this is a story held together by a collection of random coincidences, good luck and chance meetings, I don't believe anything in the world is accidental. I know we are on a Soul Journey in spiritual connection with ourselves, each other, nature and the universe. This belief of spiritual connection, is the subject of my next book: 'My Soul Path Is Connection.' How to live from the Inside.

Author Q & A

Why did you write a book about business partnerships and intimate relationships?

I wrote the book because I was sure other couples might find themselves in the same position Heather and I were in, as we were preparing to sell up and leave Sydney. Could we reawaken the intimate relationship we had just begun at the start of our journey, after ten years in business together? We had a great many issues to sort out as we tried to separate our relationship from our business partnership, and I was deeply concerned we had sacrificed our intimate relationship for the business. My fears were such I decided we needed the professional help of a couple's counsellor. I felt our story would be helpful and give hope to other couples going through the same process. Expediting ourselves from the business structure felt frightening; I felt exposed and found writing the book took me back to our beginning and helped me understand both our intimate and business journey.

Do you think most people know someone, or have been close to someone who has experienced working and being in a relationship together?

It's a typical enough business arrangement, one person has a manual or professional skill, and the partner provides the office skills, secretarial and bookkeeping. Many well-established businesses started in kitchens and garages with a committed couple working toward a common goal. While it seems obvious, not every couple can navigate the problems working and living together bring. I think the primary area for a couple to work out is how to divide the workload, so one partner doesn't feel they are shouldering the burden. The second is establishing clear communications and a method of conflict resolution that is sturdy enough in every situation, personal or business. I believe a clear understanding of the needs, vision, and direction of both the relationship and the partnership means less misunderstanding and unrealised dreams.

If people have challenges or come up against obstacles working together and being in a relationship, what would you say to help them persevere?

Communication, communication, communication with lots and lots of love, with a daily dash of humour, patience, and perseverance. I believe whatever energy and drive you bring to your business; you need to bring that same level of energy and commitment to your intimate relationship. Don't be afraid to admit you made a mistake, always applaud good work, be both a leader and a follower. Step up when your skills are needed and don't let your ego have the last word over your heart. Have a clear understanding of what you want from the relationship, your needs, your expectations, your vision for the future. Set aside time to engage with each other. Don't be frightened to rock the boat; talk about your fears as often as you talk about your hopes and dreams.

What's your wish for people once they've read your book?

To believe they can do it! On paper, Heather and I weren't a love match, unless you believe exact opposites make for a loving, healthy relationship. With our lack of experience in running a small business, in handling large numbers of dogs, you'd have been right in your scepticism and maybe predicted that we'd survive two years, not ten. Age is no barrier to moving to a new country, falling in love, starting a new business, changing your life. Give yourself space to have a new thought, a new dream, a new goal. Nothing is impossible, so set in concrete, that it can't change. Just because this is the way it's always been doesn't mean it has to stay that way. That dream, that story, that painting, that trip, it's your life, and you only have one. My wish is all those who read this book are inspired to write their own story, to share their life with others so your courage can inspire us.

What actions can people take now to help them improve their business partnership and intimate relationship?

Start a conversation today. Open the discussion with honesty, say how you feel. Talk about all the things you have been hiding, putting off, afraid to bring up in case your partner gets hurt or it makes a tense situation more uncomfortable. Confront that subject you have been hesitant to bring up. Open that can of worms and thrash out the problem, confront your fears, say what you are afraid of, even if it makes a tense situation more uncomfortable or possibly out of control. Your relationship and your business can only grow and move forward to the extent you are willing and able to grow and develop yourself. You are the only person who can take the bold steps to move through the fear that is holding you back. I believe we enter a loving relationship to learn about ourselves and for the same reason, many of us learn about who we are running a small business.

What are three pieces of wisdom you live by day to day?

My Soul Path is connection. I use daily journaling to connect with my Inner Voice, to go deep inside, to find stillness and a time of reflection, insight and mediation. This morning ritual, scribbling down my thoughts, my ideas, allowing my creativity to flow, keeps me true to my Self.

'What happens is supposed to happen'. The good or bad, fun or tragic, ups and downs, it's what is supposed to happen on our Soul Path, and it's up to us to meet the challenges life presents.

It's not about having a life with no problems. It's about how you solve the problems. I became a problem solver as part of my sobriety, and it's one of the best lessons I learnt. As an addict, I would create family and work problems because of my drinking and drug use and my behaviour, and then not know how to deal with the hostility and friction I had caused.

How do you stay motivated and inspired to do the work you do?

I'm passionate about everything I do. I have an enormous amount of personal energy, self-direction and will-power. I'm not sure that was given to me so I could survive my life or if, because of my personality, I've made my life more difficult. When I was drinking and using I did so in the most abusive manner, but I've brought that same strong resolve to my sobriety. I still have some of the addict traits; obsessional behaviour, compulsive, perfectionism, immediate need for gratification, a tendency to self-absorption, occasionally self-centred -single-mindedness when I begin a project. As Heather will attest, it's not getting me started, but trying to get me to stop. I live from the place of being spiritually connected with my Inner Self, Inner World, Inner Life. I act on my intuition, gut feelings, hunches and the quiet, whispered words in my head.

Acknowledgements

Getting up at five o'clock in the morning and leaving a warm bed was the only way I could see myself having the quiet time I needed to write. It wasn't my idea, but something I read that enabled another writer to finish her book and so I say to that early riser – "Thank you."

The idea I had for writing this book might have stayed just an idea tucked away in the back of my mind, if I hadn't chanced across Emma Franklin Bell's FREE 5-DAY BOOK PLANNING CHALLENGE. I entered the challenge and with each day my idea progressed and became more real. At the end of the challenge, I had the opportunity to speak with Emma and asked her to support my writing the book. Emma has been an amazing support through the writing; her expertise, professionalism, skill and willingness to share her experience and knowledge with honesty have made this book a hundred times superior to anything I could have written on my own. I have learnt so much, thank you Emma.

Special thanks to the love-of-my-life, my wife, business partner, Heather Collins. Without her blessing, I wouldn't have been able to tell this story, our story, and share it with other couples who have an intimate relationship and business partnership. Once again, Heather was willing to take a leap of faith with me as I began my goal to write and self-publish ten books in ten years.

Joanne and I have worked together on several projects and it was a given that I would ask her to design the book cover. As always, Joanne has created something that is eye-catching and beautiful. Thank you so much, Joanne, as always it has been a pleasure to work with you.

My editor Karen made herself known to me by commenting on my 'Soul Scribbling' Facebook posts. I was so pleased when she suggested I might contact her about the editing of my manuscript. She made the whole process very simple and I agreed immediately with her clear corrections and suggestions. Thank you, Karen.

David was an amazing find, a suggestion from a friend and I'm so glad I took up the recommendation. I will also be recommending David in the future. Thank you, David.

What is left to say about Philippe, our photographer than we haven't said and been saying over the ten years we have been working with him, he is amazing. The cover photo is a beautiful example of his magic. Thank you, Philippe.

Special Acknowledgement
RIP Esme: my first client puppy.

Resources

Passionate Marriage
Keeping love and intimacy alive in committed relationships.
By: Schnarch David

The E-Myth Revisited
Why most small businesses don't work and what to do about it.
By: Michael E Gerber

ADA Dyslexia Association Australia
Dyslexia Association Australia

Manuscript Mastery Book Coaching

Emma has filled the pages of journals and notebooks since she was a young girl, and this sparked her desire to help others unearth and share their own stories and words of wisdom. Supporting and guiding people to write their story, share their insights and share their lived experiences energises Emma

to the core. Writing and sharing your words is powerful and meaningful and Emma's vision is to help you see what's possible when it comes to getting your ideas out of your head and into a book you can share with the world.
https://emmafranklinbell.com/

Joanne Tapodi Creative

For Joanne design is more than her day job – it's a way of life. She is inspired by everything around her, and because she is lucky enough to do what she loves, it's something that's reflected in her work. It's a fantastic feeling to be part of a client's dream project and to share that exciting journey with them. Joanne's ultimate goal is assisting clients in creating a brand that they can be proud of, a brand that is a stand-out success and achieves their unique vision and values.
https://www.joannetapodicreative.com.au/

Exact Editing

Karen Crombie runs *Exact Editing*, where the aim is to make your work shine. Working at Buckingham Palace for the Queen took her natural eye for detail to a new level, bringing a meticulous standard to her editing work. Karen brings her skill with the written word to articles, website copy, blogs and book manuscripts. She can spot a spelling error across a crowded restaurant and loves clever wordplay and bad puns.
Find her on Facebook; **https://www.facebook.com/ExactEditing/**
Or the *Exact Editing* website; **https://exactediting.com.au/**

David James Lawton

For David, graphic design was something of a major career change, having started out in the world of accounting and finance. Now a designer for over sixteen years, David began with five years in-house experience at Cambridge

University Press before establishing his own business. Regarding this as his best career decision, it has given David the opportunity to work with a diverse range of clients from all over the world, embracing the daily creative challenges that this presents.
https://davidjameslawton.com/

Image Technique

Philippe loves helping people tell their story through photographs that capture their warmth, energy and spirit. Raised in a family that cherished photos, Philippe developed a fascination with the medium from an early age. In 2007 Philippe's passion led to him launching his studio, *Image Technique Photography* in Sydney's Inner West, Marrickville, where he first met Hannah and Heather Collins.

"It has been an absolute privilege to photograph Hannah and Heather over the years, telling their personal story together, capturing their wedding and also providing promotional photography for their pet business."
https://imagetechnique.com.au/

About The Author

Hannah began her writing career at twelve self-publishing her first book about four children and their dog, reminiscent of Enid Blyton's 'The Famous Five'. Her mother typed up the papers and helped make a cardboard cover, with a hand-drawn illustration, from an empty Weetbix box. She followed this up by winning her first literary prize, a beautiful green fountain pen, awarded by a representative of the Canadian Tourist Board, for her school holiday project, an illustrated booklet entitled 'Why I Want To Visit Canada'.

As a young, divorced mother of two children, Hannah joined the Women's Electoral Lobby and became politically active in the Women's Movement. Hannah has written for political journals, broadsheets, magazines and newsletters.

Escaping Auckland and moving to Nelson when her sons were teenagers, Hannah began to journal her experiences from 'Coming Out' and her five years in a lesbian, domestic violence relationship.

Recovering from a nervous breakdown and admitting to years of alcohol and drug abuse, Hannah went into rehab to deal with her childhood sexual abuse, dysfunctional family patterns and co-dependent relationship behaviour.

It was while she was living on the land, under the mountains in the backblocks of New Zealand's South Island, without electricity or running water and working with horses, that Hannah reawakened her spirituality, her Pagan beliefs, and her Inner Voice.

Writing became the creative force that allowed Hannah to examine her life in minute detail, to move beyond the Outer Life and, with sensitive introspection and insight, gain wisdom from her pain. Her daily journaling detailed her Inner Life, her short stories about life on the land, the horses, and back to nature lifestyle gained attention from magazines, and Radio New Zealand's national program. Her self-published poetry and short stories featured in 'Nelson Writers' anthologies.

To celebrate her tenth year of sobriety, Hannah self-published a collection of short stories that represented each year of her recovery, along with an exhibition of ten mixed-media pieces.

Hannah's most ambitious book launch was for her collection of poetry 'Reflections In A Puddle', in collaboration with three local artists; a toymaker, a sculptor, a photographer, and the debut performance from a woman's band.

About The Author

When Hannah and Heather went into the dog walking and pet sitting business, Hannah continued to write, managing the social media marketing, newsletter and self-publishing a 'How-To book' on dog grooming.

In 2018 Hannah launched 'Soul Scribbling' an online membership site for 'Crones', women who have reached that stage of life where they want to connect, through writing, with their Inner Voice, their Inner Self.

Hannah has a goal over the next decade; to write and self-publish ten books. This is her first offering *In Business Together: Negotiating the intimate relationship and the business partnership.*
Enjoy!

Connect With The Author

Website
https://hannahcollins.com.au

Facebook
https://www.facebook.com/hannahsoulscribbling

Thinkific
https://soulscribblinghannah.thinkific.com/

Free Online Course – Journaling 101

Hi, Hannah here, inviting you to join my foundation Journaling Course. I want to share with you how much you can gain and learn about yourself when you spend as little as 15 minutes each day writing down your thoughts and feelings in your special journaling notebook.

I've been using daily journaling for over three decades, and it has been the tool I used to change my life from being a homeless alcoholic living in a van on the side of the road, to becoming a successful business owner and author.

Journaling can be a powerful tool for change, for connecting with your Inner Voice and finding your wisdom, self-confidence and repairing the damage that might be holding you back or stopping you from loving and caring for yourself.

We all have an Outer World and an Inner World. Most of us are very aware of our Outer World; it is our World since birth. The Outer World has labels about us; female, girl, woman, daughter, mother, gardener, teacher, businesswoman. For some, the Inner World is no more than a voice buzzing in our head that we choose to ignore.

Journaling is about a connection to this Inner World, to listening to that Inner Voice, to paying attention and being self-aware. To learn who you are, your authentic Self. This journey of self-discovery is a life-long journey, and through your journaling, you can find your wisdom, be your inspiration, be self-directed not looking outside for approval and permission to act. You can discover your spirituality and walk your Soul Path.

In this course, I want to inspire you to write in your journal every day. To start a practice of life extended writing, to connect with your Inner Voice and have access to the deepest, most personal and intimate part of yourself. To find your inner truth and to live your life the best way you know, by your values, your experiences, your truth.

We start journaling the same way we begin any journey - by doing! Join today here: **https://soulscribblinghannah.thinkific.com/manage/courses**

FREE online Course – Journaling 101

What you will receive:

- Chapter 1   Journaling
  - Lesson 1   Introduction to Journaling
  - Lesson 2   Why Journaling
  - Lesson 3   What is the difference between Journaling and keeping a diary?

Chapter 2 Notebooks and pencils
    Lesson 4 A Journal and Pen

Chapter 3 Your Inner Voice
    Lesson 5 What Is Your Inner Voice
    Lesson 6 Connection with your Inner Voice

Chapter 4 Getting Started
    Lesson 7 How often do I write, when do I write and what do I write
    Lesson 8 Why writing by hand

Chapter 5 Journaling Ideas
    Lesson 9 Tips & tricks to get you started

Chapter 6 How will Journaling change my life
    Lesson 10 My Story
    Lesson 11 Your Story

Plus a special bonus gift:

Sign up for your FREE Journaling course here

https://soulscribblinghannah.thinkific.com/

www.ingramcontent.com/pod-product-compliance
Lightning Source LLC
Chambersburg PA
CBHW020323010526
44107CB00054B/1960